STAGECRAFT FOR NONPROFESSIONALS

KEY TO PARTS OF THE STAGE

1 Act Curtain
2 Portal
3 Footlights
4 Legs
5 Backdrop
6 Fire Doors
7 Sheaves
8 Head Blocks
9 Gridiron
10 Batten
11 Pin Rail
12 First Border Light
13 Spotlight Batten
14 Smoke Pocket

15 Counterweight
16 Switchboard
17 Lock Rail
18 Sand Bag
19 Asbestos Curtain
20 Operating Line Act Curtain
21 Operating Line Asbestos
22 Second Border Light
23 Third Border Light
24 Floor Tension Sheaves
25 Proscenium Wall
26 Proscenium Opening
27 Border
28 Fly Floor

STAGECRAFT

FOR

NONPROFESSIONALS

by F. A. BUERKI

THE UNIVERSITY OF WISCONSIN PRESS

Published 1955, 1972
The University of Wisconsin Press
Box 1379, Madison, Wisconsin 53701

The University of Wisconsin Press, Ltd.
70 Great Russell Street, London

Third Edition 1972

Printed in the United States of America
ISBN 0-299-06234-1, LC 72-2883

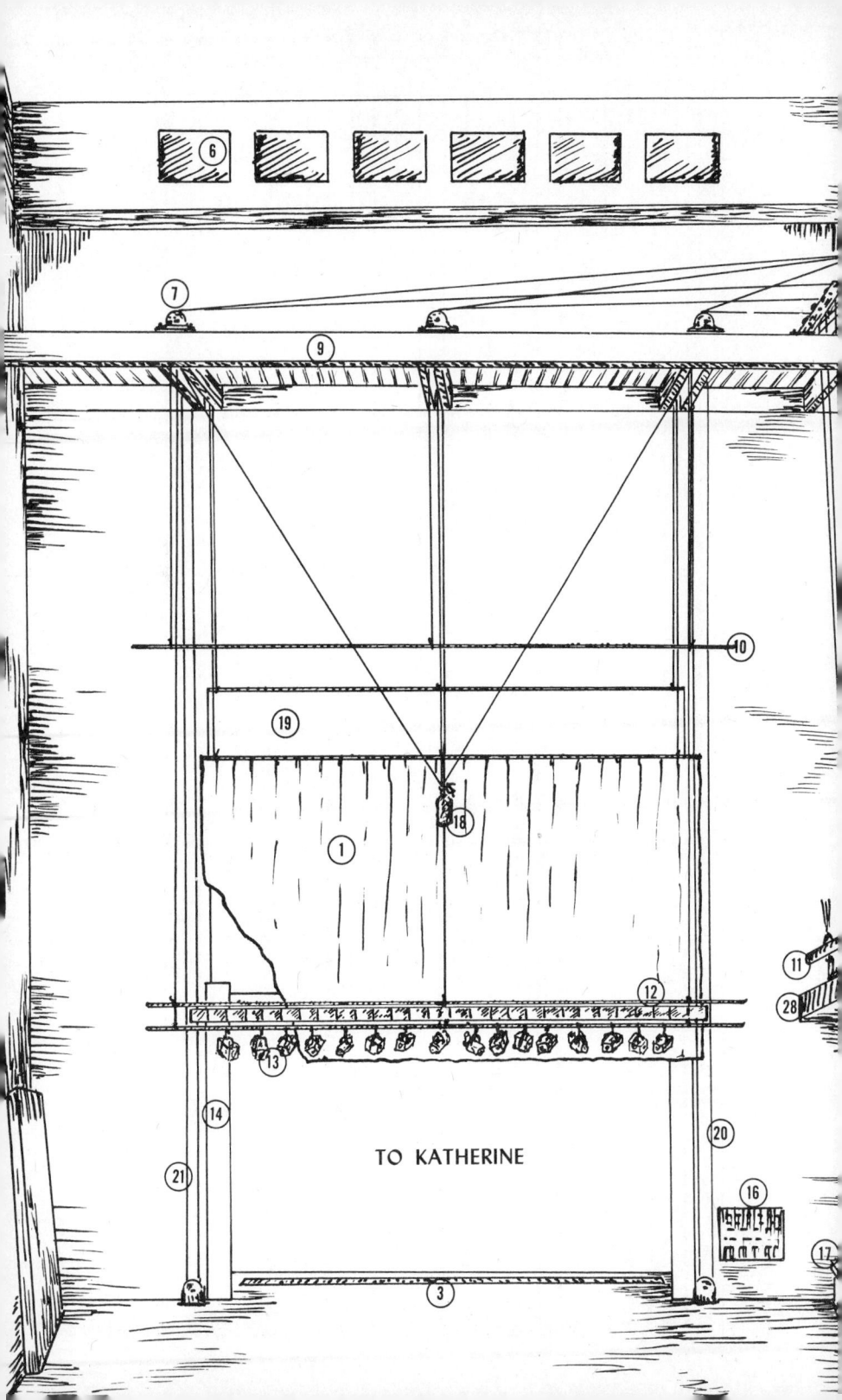

TO KATHERINE

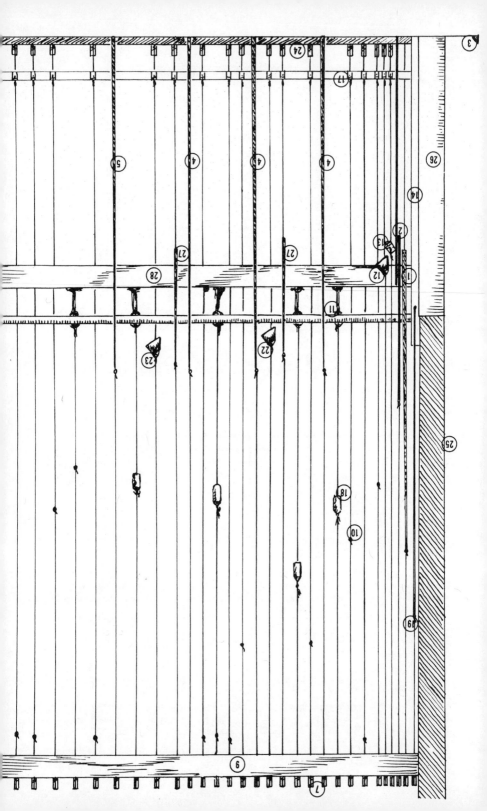

PREFACE

The teaching of dramatic arts in secondary schools and colleges is in a measure responsible for the development of a new nonprofessional theatre. To students and faculties in high schools and colleges and to community leaders who are interested in this new nonprofessional theatre this book is offered with the hope that it may aid in the solution of production problems and stimulate a new and greater interest in stagecraft.

For those amateurs who are interested in building, painting, and lighting scenery for schools and little theatres, simple, practical information is not readily available. There are books on scenic arts, but they are either too theoretical or too involved for the nonprofessional's use. This book endeavors to present a simple, concise, yet technical discussion of stagecraft. Much that might have been included about the stage has been omitted purposely, because it is of such an involved and technical nature that it would be highly impractical. Many suggestions made in the following pages may not correspond to professional methods and practices. They are made for reasons of economy and simplicity and, it is hoped, in the best interest of the nonprofessional stage craftsman.

F. A. BUERKI

Madison, Wisconsin
March, 1955

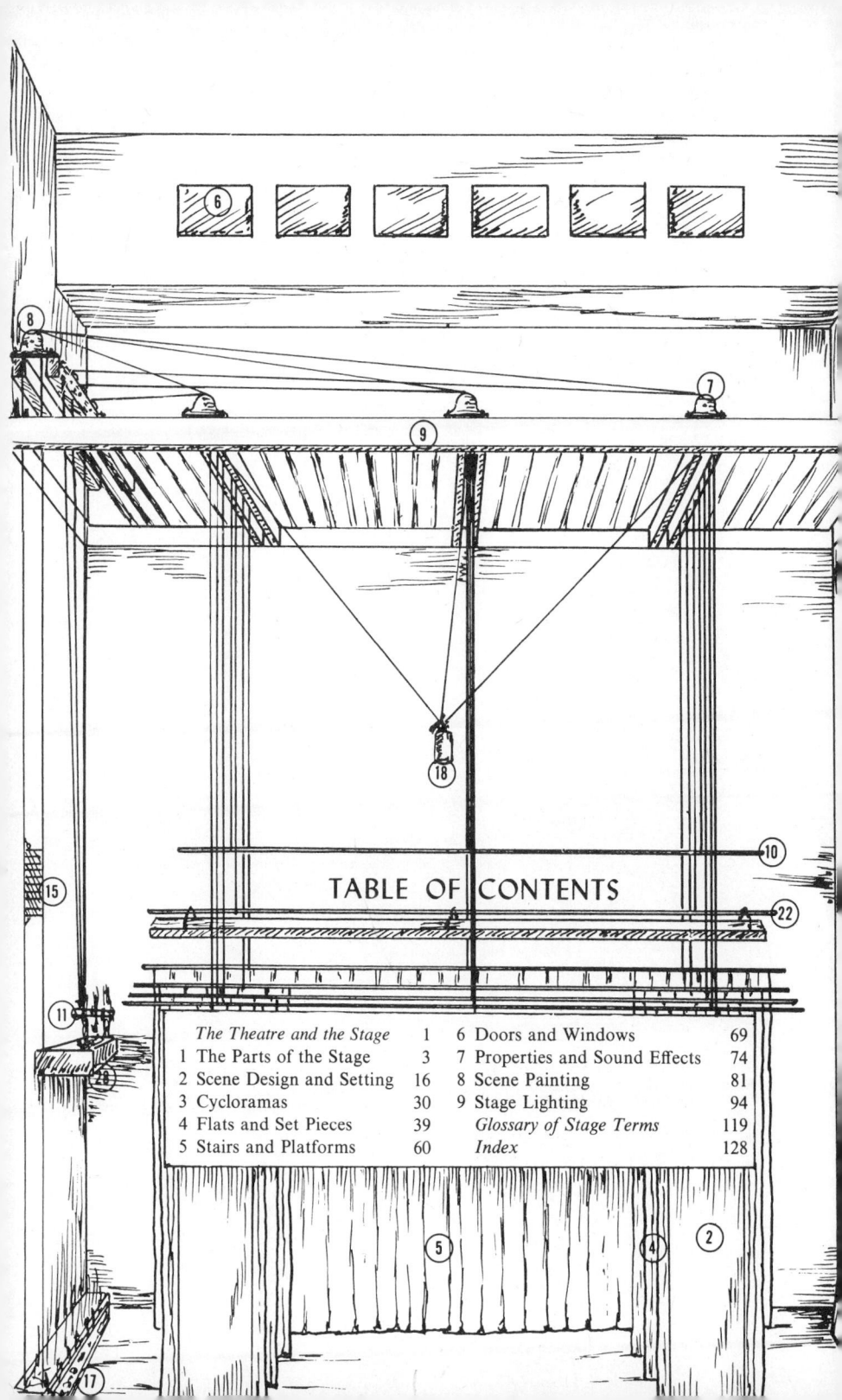

TABLE OF CONTENTS

LIST OF ILLUSTRATIONS

THE THEATRE AND THE STAGE

Theatres take many forms, but the operation of the stage or the building, painting and lighting of its scenery are primarily the same for all of them. The most common form of the theatre is the proscenium stage, sometimes referred to as the Italian Renaissance theatre because that is where and when it was originated. The audience in this theatre is seated opposite a picture-frame type of opening, watching an action on a raised platform back of the frame. There are several other well-defined types of audience-actor relationships. Theatre-in-the-round or arena staging is early Greek in origin. The action occurs on a central raised area completely surrounded by the audience. Actors enter and exit through radial aisles. Open- or end-staging is also Greek in origin. The audience is seated opposite an open, raised platform. A third form is the thrust stage, generally attributed to Elizabethan Shakespearean England. In this form, the stage projects into the auditorium, with the audience seated in a horseshoe shape around the action. This stage may be backed by a proscenium with a complete stage behind the opening.

Stage machinery and scenery are more important in the proscenium theatre than they are in the other three forms, while lighting is frequently emphasized in the thrust, open, and arena stages. But some form of scenery is often required for these stages as well. When scenery is used for any stage, the methods of construction and painting are basically the same for all. Although this book is primarily gauged to proscenium production, the suggestions that follow are equally valid for any type of theatre.

1

I

THE PARTS OF THE STAGE

BASIC EQUIPMENT

A theatre is composed of two main parts. The portion in front of the curtain, which normally comprises the seating area, lobbies, box offices, and lounges, is for the use and convenience of the audience. The portion back of the curtain is composed of the stage, or stage house, dressing room, or dressing room facilities, and, in some instances, shops for building and painting scenery and for making costumes, and space for storage.

Apron

The stage floor extending forward from the curtain line to the front of the stage platform is the apron or forestage. At one time this area was very large, but later it became small and unimportant. Recently the forestage has reappeared in the form of an orchestra pit that may be floored over at stage level to create a thrust stage. Frequently the dual-purpose orchestra pit thrust stage is accomplished through the use of a forestage elevator. This elevator at auditorium floor level may also be used for additional seating.

Switchboard

Directly inside the proscenium arch, on stage right or left, or in a booth at the rear of the auditorium, is located the switchboard for the control of the stage lights.

Pin Rail

At one side of the stage, preferably on the switchboard side—usually called the prompt side—is a pin rail, which may be located on the floor or above the stage on a bridge (called the fly gallery) that runs from the front to the back wall. The pin rail is a 6 by 6 timber bolted to the wall about 3 feet from the floor and held 6 to 8 inches away from the wall with blocks. (See Figure 2.) A 6-inch pipe may

3

also be used as a pin rail. Holes are drilled vertically through the timber or pipe, into which wood or iron pins are dropped. A flange, or collar, about halfway down the pin prevents it from dropping too far through the rail. When in position, the pin projects about 6 inches above and below the rail. Around this pin are tied the ropes that are used to raise or lower the suspended scenery, as shown in Figure 1.

Pin rails are not always attached to the wall. Frequently they are placed away from the wall so that the flyman can stand behind the rail facing the stage. In this case the rail is mounted on wood or metal supports from the floor, as shown in Figure 2. This is always true on a fly gallery.

Fly Gallery

A fly gallery (see Figure 3) runs along the side wall of the stage from front to back, not less than 16 feet above the stage floor. The pin rail is then located on the fly gallery. This arrangement saves floor space for scenery and leaves free wall space against which to stack scenery that is not being used. A fly gallery has many disadvantages, however, especially on a stage with a small and inexperienced crew. The difference in levels makes it impossible to double-up the duties of the stage crew, and it is often necessary to have a crew both on the stage floor and in the fly gallery.

Gridiron

Just beneath the stage ceiling or roof the grid, or gridiron, is lo-

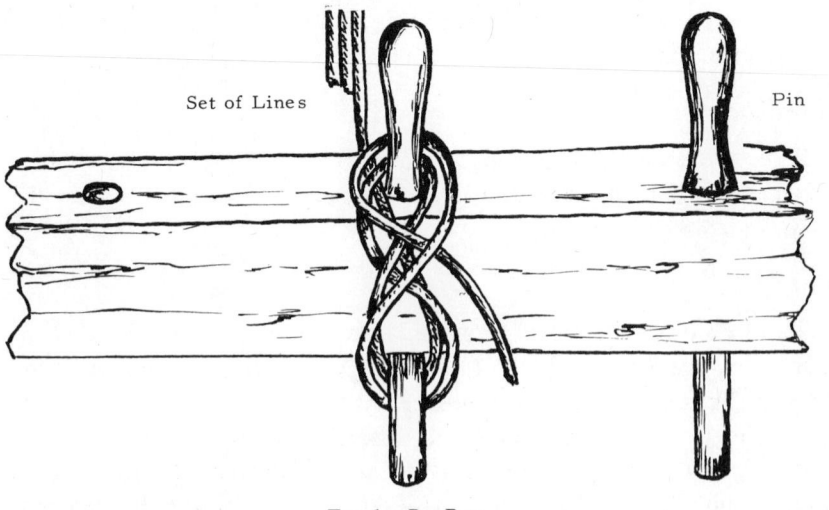

Set of Lines   Pin

Fig. 1.—Pin Rail

cated. There should be some space between the grid and the roof to allow a man to work with some ease for the necessary adjustments of lines and rigging. Three feet is sufficient, more is desirable. The gridiron is a network of steel beams on which rest sheaves or loft blocks—a special form of pulley. (See Figure 4.)

Set of Lines

Over these sheaves pass the ropes that run from the scenery to the pin rail. Usually these ropes and sheaves are arranged in sets of three, as shown in Figure 4. These three ropes are called a set of lines. The lines start at the pin rail and pass up to the grid and over the first set of sheaves, called the head block—three sheaves set side by side or one sheave above the other. Then the ropes pass over single sheaves and down to the floor. The rope that passes over the sheave nearest the head block is called the short line. The next rope, which goes over the sheave above the center of the stage, is called the center line. The rope that passes over the third sheave on the side of the stage opposite the head block is called the long line. These three lines that reach to the stage floor are tied to a batten or to a piece of scenery.

Battens

A batten, in this instance, may be a 1-inch or a 1½-inch pipe, or

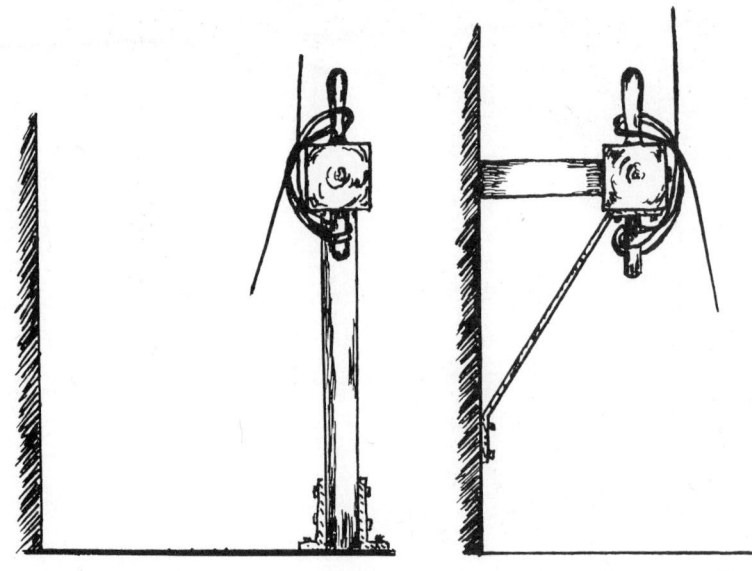

FIG. 2.—PIN RAIL MOUNTED ON THE WALL (RIGHT) AND BUILT UP FROM THE FLOOR (LEFT)

it may be two pieces of 1 by 3 inch lumber nailed or screwed together. To the batten, scenery is tied or attached. A clovehitch, shown in Figure 4, is the type of knot best suited for tying ropes to battens.

When the batten is not in actual use, it may be removed, and the three rope ends may be tied to a canvas bag filled with sand. The sand bag is then pulled up out of the way. The bag keeps the ropes from running on through the sheaves and serves as a weight to pull the ropes back to the floor when they are needed.

When there is no grid, sheaves or pulleys may be attached directly to the ceiling. When it is impossible to do even this, large screw eyes may be put into the ceiling and the battens attached to the screw eyes with large harness or rope snaps.

Counterweight Systems

A more elaborate method of flying or raising scenery is found in the counterweight system. This arrangement, however, if installed exclusively on a stage has many disadvantages. Counterweight sys-

FIG. 3.—FLY GALLERY

tems are not as flexible as rope sets. Counterweighted sets have battens of fixed length and of fixed trim. (The term "trim" is used to indicate that any hanging piece is in its proper place—level, at the correct height, or covering other objects not to be seen.) All three lines must be used at all times, since they are permanently attached to a batten.

The principle of counterweighting a fire curtain is shown in Figure 5. Other counterweighted sets are similar in principle, with but one additional device. Just above the floor sheave there is a locking device located on a lock rail to hold the pull line. This keeps the scenery at any desired position even if the balance between the counterweight and the scenery is not perfect. The lock rail runs parallel to the pin rail but is almost always on the stage floor.

With rope sets, the battens may vary in length according to requirements, the trim may be quickly changed, and any one line may be used separately. An ideal arrangement for a stage is a combination of both types of flying. If only one type is available, the simple arrangement of the lines and pin rail is more flexible, but a counterweight system is easier to operate. A stage should have a set of lines from 6 inches to 1 foot apart from the proscenium to the back wall.

STAGE CURTAINS

Well-equipped stages should have at least two curtains: a fire cur-

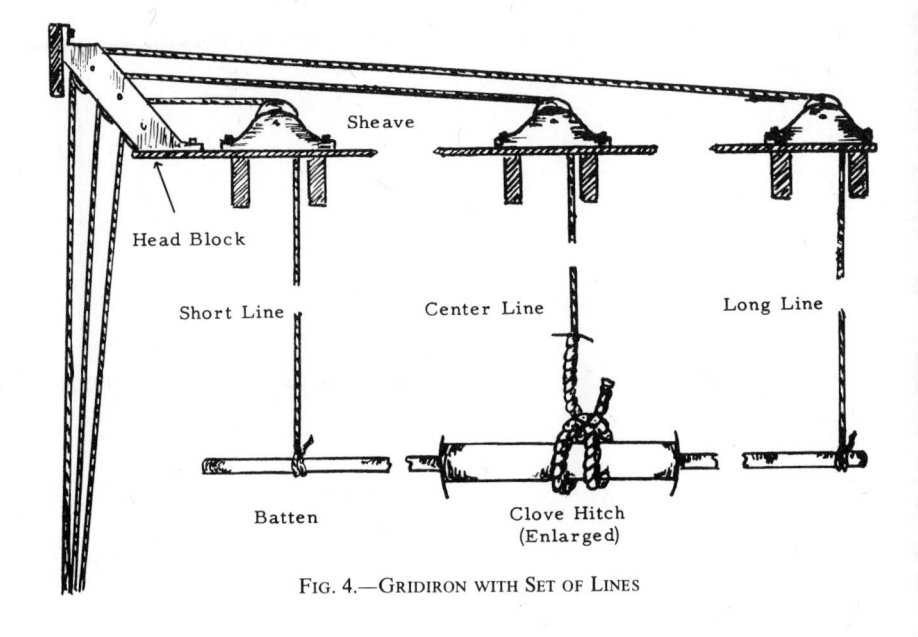

FIG. 4.—GRIDIRON WITH SET OF LINES

tain for emergencies and a working curtain, or act curtain, to be used before and after acts or scenes. Curtains are discussed here following an explanation of pin rails, lock rails, sets of lines, and counter-weighted sets because they are dependent on this rigging for their operation.

Automatic Fire Curtain

A fire curtain is required by state law in all professional theatres, and though some schools and little theatres have been exempt from

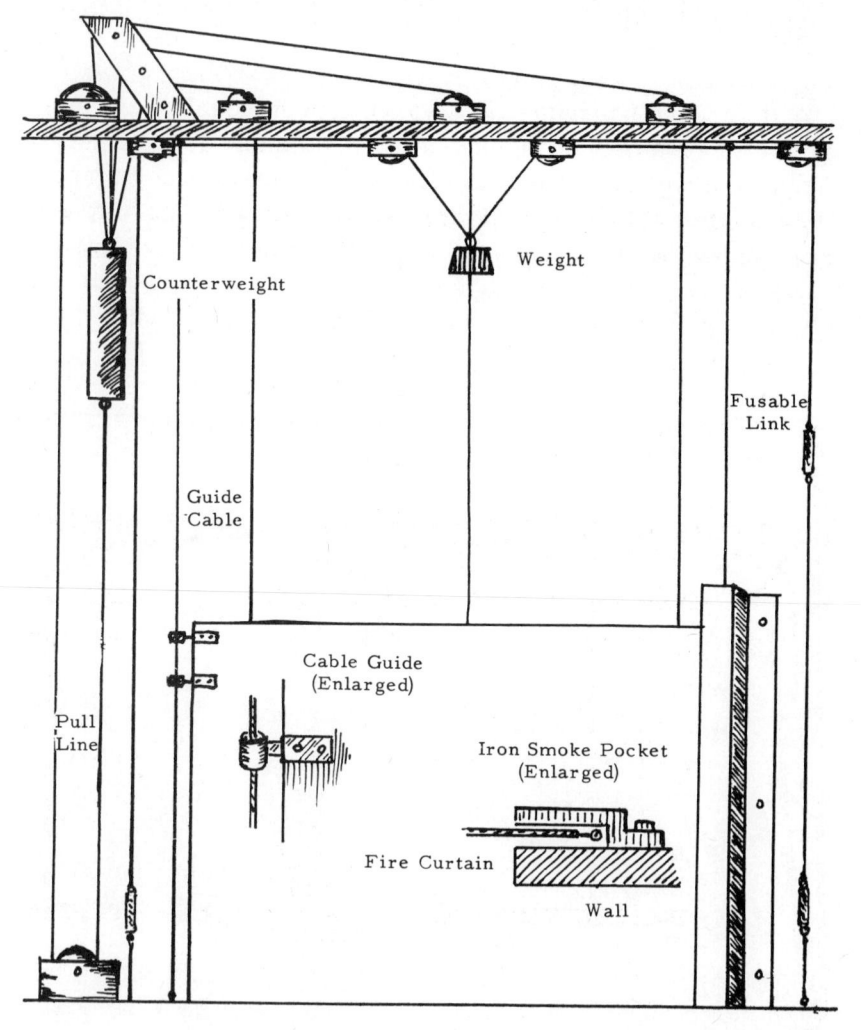

FIG. 5.—COUNTERWEIGHTING THE FIRE CURTAIN

this requirement they are gradually being asked to comply with the law. A fire curtain, or asbestos as it is usually called, is made of some fireproof material such as asbestos and is located directly inside the proscenium arch. The fire curtain travels in a smoke pocket made of boilerplate iron which is bolted directly to the proscenium arch.

Because of its great weight the fire curtain is always counterweighted—that is, the rope by which it is raised and lowered has attached to it weights almost equal to that of the curtain. This arrangement makes it possible for a person to operate the asbestos with little effort.

A fire curtain should be arranged so that in addition to its manual operation it will close automatically in case of fire. This automatic closing device is very simple. A light rope or sash cord is run up both sides of the proscenium wall. These ropes join in the center above the asbestos curtain and suspend weight sufficiently heavy to overbalance the counterweight of the curtain. In several places this rope is cut and held together with fusable links—small metal plates which melt at a very low temperature. In case of fire these links melt, the weight drops onto the curtain, and the curtain closes. (See Figure 5.) This curtain should be raised a few minutes before the show begins and lowered after the performance is over.

Act, or Working, Curtain

The act, or working, curtain may operate in several ways. The common types are guillotine, traveller, and opera drape. The traveller opens from side to side; the opera drape loops up on both sides of center; and the guillotine raises and lowers. A curtain may also roll up from the bottom, but this type should be used only for special occasions, such as, for instance, in the revival of the old melodrama. In the period of the melodrama the curtain which rolled from the bottom was quite common, but it is now obsolete. The guillotine, opera drape, and the traveller are so commonly used that it will be advisable to describe their operations.

Guillotine.—The guillotine curtain operates on exactly the same principle as the fire curtain. It is attached to a set of lines and raised and lowered with the aid of counterweight. The principal differences between the two operations are that the guillotine curtain is not equipped with an automatic fire device and that the guillotine curtain does not run in a smoke pocket. The counterweight and the guillotine curtain are in perfect balance in order to facilitate smooth and easy raising and lowering. The operating line is either heavy jute or braided cotton. A hemp rope should never be used. It is affected by the weather, it shrinks and stretches, and, furthermore, it is slivery and hard on the hands. The guillotine type of curtain is most commonly used in legitimate theatres.

Opera drape.—The opera drape is a two-piece curtain open in the center. On the back of the curtain from both lower center corners diagonally up to the upper right and left corners a series of rings are sewn, one at each seam. Pulleys are fastened to each end of the batten to which the curtain is attached, a double pulley on the side from which the curtain is to be operated, a single pulley on the other side. A rope is attached to the lower center ring on the side of the single pulley and threaded up through each of the rings to the single pulley and across the top to the double pulley. The rope is then dropped to the floor and taken back up to the other half of the double pulley. The rope is finally threaded down through the other set of rings and attached to the other lower center corner. (See Figure 6.)

If the rope at the side is pulled properly, the curtains will open evenly. The weight of the curtains is usually sufficient to make them close by themselves. Sometimes, however, it is necessary to have weights in the lower center corner to make the curtains close completely. The curtain shown in Figure 6 is the simplest form of opera

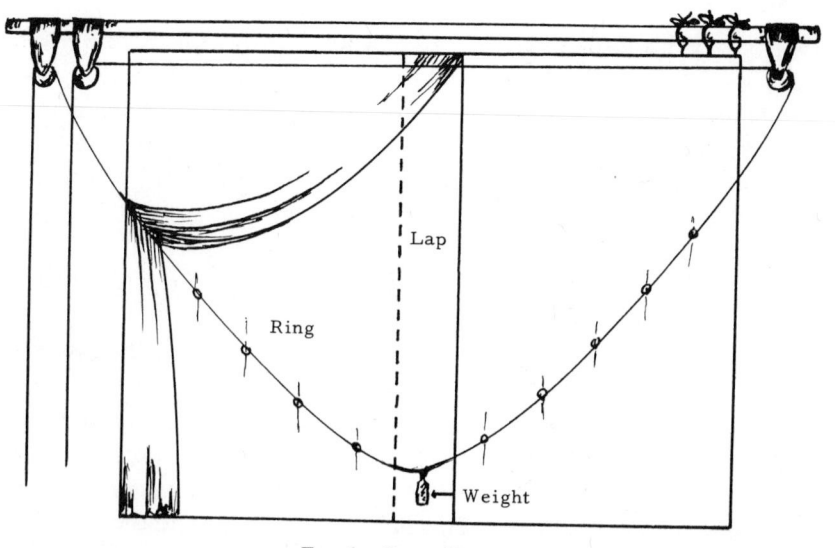

FIG. 6.—OPERA DRAPE

drape. An opera drape should be sufficiently high, wide, and full so that when it is opened it will not draw up at the outside, or right and left off-stage corners.

A braided clothesline or sash cord will do as a rope for opening and closing the curtains. If the opera drape is very heavy, a special ½ inch braided cotton cord is best. Opera drapes are used as working curtains for certain types of productions for which an air of elegance is required. They are frequently used also at other places on the stage for revealing tableaux and inner scenes. The principle of the opera drape applies to the looping up of draperies in doorways.

The traveller on a wire track.—All travellers must operate from some kind of track. Although there are many types of tracks, the principle on which they operate is the same. Two of the simplest types of tracks are described here.

The simplest traveller operates on one or, preferably, two heavy, smooth wires. (See Figure 7.) The two halves of the curtain are hung from the wire by rings or S-hooks that will slide easily along the wire. (A pipe may be used in place of wire, provided the pipe is made up of not more than two pieces joined at the center.) The wires are stretched across the stage and drawn tight with turnbuckles. When two wires are used, the wires should not be more than six inches apart. With two wires it is possible for the curtains to lap over as they close. With one wire, it is almost impossible to make the curtain close completely.

If one wire is used, a support may be dropped from above to hold up the center. With two wires, two supports are attached, one to each wire, one about a foot to the right of center, and the other about a foot to the left of center.

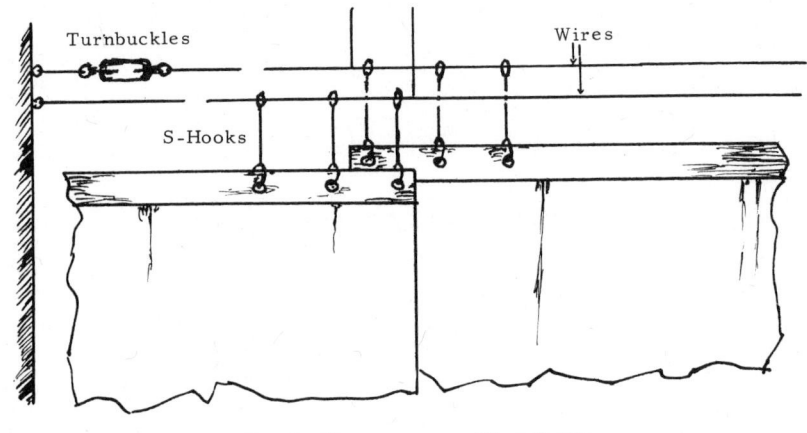

FIG. 7.—TRAVELLER ON A WIRE TRACK

The traveller on a wood track.—The type of traveller commonly used is the wood track shown in Figure 8, although tracks are also made of steel. The wood track is approximately 4 inches square. It is a long hollow box at least 4 feet longer than the proscenium opening. It is constructed in two sections, with one section overlapping the other 2 or 3 feet at the center. The top and sides of the track are solid; the bottom has a narrow slit the full length of the box. (See Figure 8.) Wood traveller balls or blocks slide back and forth in the hollow space—about 1½ inches square—of the traveller.

Each block has a hole drilled in its center, through which a heavy piece of wire is passed. One end of the wire is riveted or bent so that it will not pull through the block. The other end projects from the block several inches and is bent into an eye, from which the curtain is suspended. As the blocks or balls move back and forth in the traveller, the curtain opens and closes. Tracks are constructed in many variations of this simple principle.

Both the wood and the wire tracks are arranged with a pull-off line of the design shown in Figure 9. Both types must have a single pulley or sheave at one end and a double at the other, just as for the opera drape. In addition, there should be a pulley or sheave on the floor at the pull-off side for the line to run through. This pulley holds the rope tight and keeps it from twisting.

To arrange the line, the curtain must be closed. One end of the line is secured tightly to the upper center corner of the curtain on the side of the single sheave. The line goes from there to the single sheave and

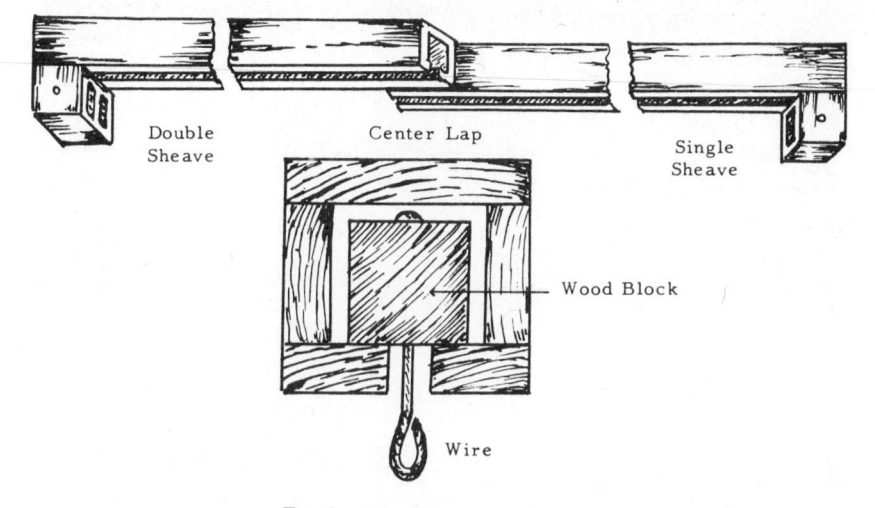

Double
Sheave

Center Lap

Single
Sheave

Wood Block

Wire

FIG. 8.—WOOD TRAVELLER TRACK

back to the center. Then the line is attached to the upper center corner of the other curtain. This line must be reasonably tight. The line then passes to one of the double sheaves and down to the floor sheave. From there it passes back up to the other double sheave and across to the center where the two ends are joined. It is important that all the slack be taken out of the rope at this point. The curtain will open by pulling one rope and close by pulling the other rope. Heavy braided cotton cord is also used in this operation.

This type of curtain is common in high school and small community theatres. It is used also as an inner curtain in professional productions. The principle of operation applies to draw curtains at windows.

Grand Drapery and Teaser

Between the asbestos and the working curtain there must be a drape. It is usually the same color and material as the working curtain. This drape should be hung on a set of lines so that it can be raised or lowered to regulate the height of the proscenium opening. This is called the grand, or the grand drapery. (See Figure 10.) Back of the working curtain about 3 feet there may be another drape, called the teaser. This also may be raised or lowered to regulate the height of the stage opening.

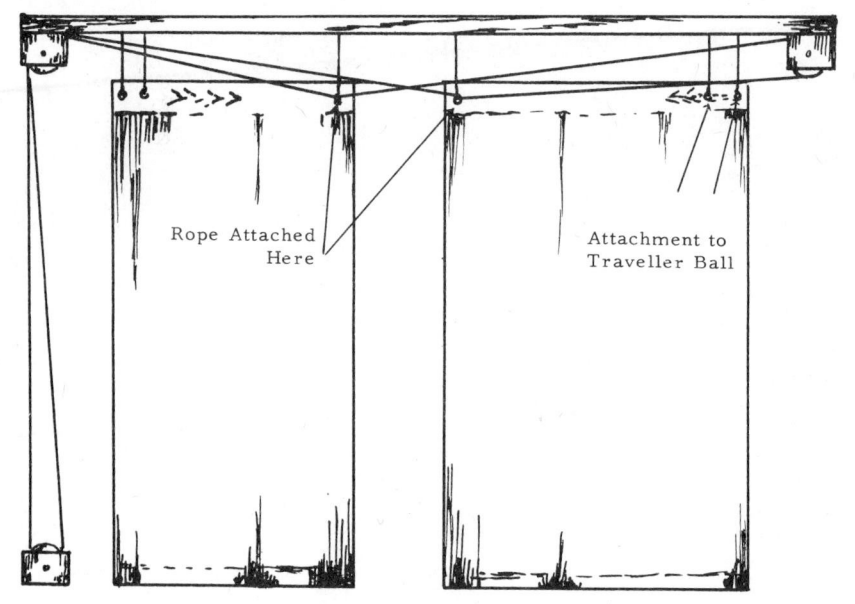

Rope Attached Here

Attachment to Traveller Ball

FIG. 9.—TRAVELLER PULL-OFF RIGGING

Tormentors and Returns

In addition, a stage should have either tormentors or returns, in some instances both. (See Figure 10.) A tormentor is made of two pieces of scenery that are hinged together. One piece starts at the proscenium and sets up and down stage. This piece is 3 or 4 feet wide, and may include a doorway, which is usually draped. The other piece sets off and on stage. The width of this section depends to some degree upon the size of the stage.

A return is a single flat of scenery set off and on stage.

The purpose of tormentors and returns is to regulate the width of the stage opening and to serve as a starting point for setting the scenery. Tormentors are more satisfactory if the stage is large or if a vaudeville type of performance is to be given. Returns are best suited to a small stage and legitimate plays. In either case, tormentors or returns together with the teaser form a second inner "picture frame," or false proscenium, for the stage.

Portals

In many instances the false proscenium, more commonly known as the portal, is not made with tormentors, returns, or teasers, but is a special piece of scenery. The portal is often designed as part of

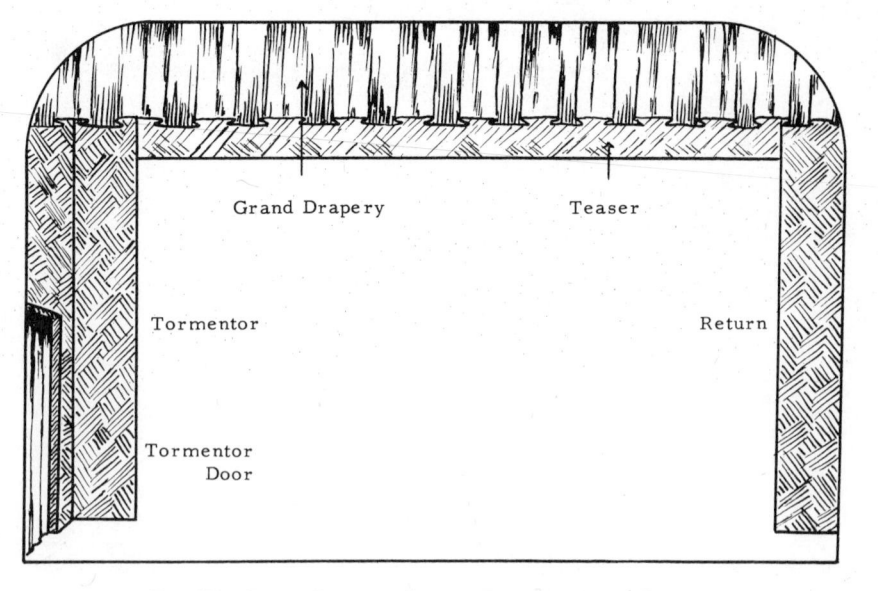

FIG. 10.—GRAND DRAPERY, TEASER, TORMENTOR, AND RETURN

the scenery for the production and serves as a specialized picture frame.

However, many portals consist of three simple frames, two sides and a top, which can be moved in and out, up and down. Portals of this type are simple scenery frames covered with black or neutral-colored cloth, usually velour or duvetyn. The upper portal frame is hung on the first set of lines back of the working curtain. (See Figure 11.) This gives control of the size and shape of the opening without the use of conventional grand drapery, tormentors, etc.

The Olio

Back of the inner picture frame there may be another curtain—guillotine, traveller, or opera drape. In this location a curtain is called an olio. This name is derived from the between-scene acts which at one time were presented in front of this curtain. The acts were called olios, a term probably derived from the Spanish word *ollà-podrida,* meaning hodgepodge.

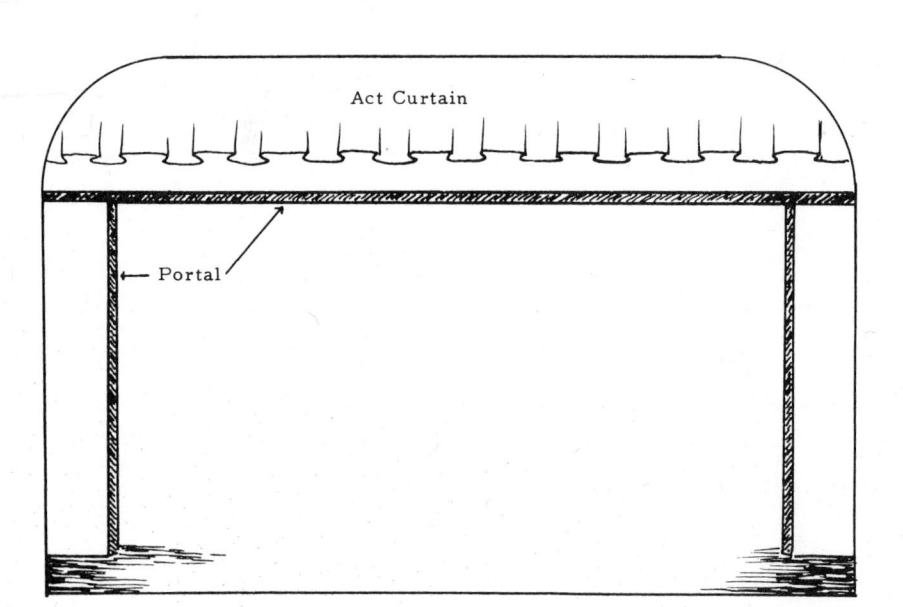

FIG. 11.—PORTAL

2

SCENE DESIGN AND SETTING

TYPES OF DESIGN

Types of scene design and classification are so numerous that it is necessary to reduce this discussion to a very few simple terms. For this reason, stage design will be divided into three general types as follows: realistic, impressionistic, and expressionistic. Other classifications might serve equally well, but few could be simpler. Perhaps no given set belongs entirely in any one of these categories but may combine features of all three.

Realistic

Realistic settings are stage settings which try to present on the stage photographic realism or reproduction of things as they actually appear, with little or no regard for artistic selectivity. Although there are many examples of this type of setting, perhaps the one most frequently cited is the scene in Child's Restaurant from Belasco's *The Governor's Lady*. Realism here was carried to the point of frying griddle cakes in a restaurant window.

Impressionistic

Impressionistic settings are settings in which careful selection has been made from real surroundings with the idea of presenting an impression of fundamental essentials, leaving much of the irrelevant and the detail to be supplied by the imagination. In this manner, scenery becomes simple and expressive, because it eliminates unnecessary detail, which often results in lack of artistic unity and strength. An example of this type of setting may be found in Claude Bragdon's sets for *Cyrano*.

Expressionistic

Expressionistic scenery has no definite relation to reality. It is either a mental expression of the idea basic to the play or an expression of the emotions of some one of the characters in the play. Settings that express ideas of this nature help to reinforce the idea or mood which the play wishes to convey. This type of setting is exemplified in Lee Simonson's designs for Elmer Rice's *The Adding Machine*.

THE DESIGN PROCESS

After this brief consideration of types of scenery it is essential to consider the more practical aspect of planning settings. This will not take the form of a discussion of scene design. An extensive discussion might be presented at this point on rhythm, balance, color, light and shade, line, form, etc., but such discussion may be found in books that deal specifically with these subjects. They have their place in scene design, but they are not prime essentials to the actual mechanics of building scenery.

Design, Light, and Color

However, at the time a set is designed attention should be given to the color and the light to be used. Both are determined by the type of play to be presented. For example, comedy requires bright light with a set in light colors; serious drama commonly is played with less illumination and in settings which are somewhat subdued in tone. The setting and the lighting add to the mood of the play. (For suggestions on lighting, see Chapter 9.)

More important than design, color, and light is the fact that a setting is required for the play that is to be presented. How is the set to be designed—or, rather, how, out of what is available to the average nonprofessional group, is a set to be assembled? Granted that design, both in principle and in application, is valuable, most producing groups are faced not so much with the problem of design as with the problem of how to make the most of the least. In creating a stage set the following approach to the problem may prove helpful.

Steps in Planning a Set

1. Have definitely in mind the stage on which the play is to be presented.

2. List the scenery available as it is and the scenery that can be rebuilt easily.

3. Know exactly to what extent new scenery may be built with the time, money, and ability available.

4. With the above three points in mind, read what the author says about the set and study the floor plan or any pictures of the play that may be available.

5. Read the play carefully, trying to create a mental picture of the setting as it might be created out of the material available for the stage on which the play is to be presented.

6. With the play well in mind, draw a floor plan that will fit the stage, that will incorporate all the essentials required in the action of the play, and that will keep within the limits of available resources, both as to possible stage mechanics and finances.

7. Draw a plan showing not only doors and windows but indicating also how the set is to be made up of separate pieces of scenery. (See Figure 12.)

8. Make a sketch showing the set as it will actually appear when ready for use.

9. Mark each piece of scenery to show whether it is old, rebuilt, or new. If the scenery to be used is readily available and if the stage is free, it is advisable to set up the scenery in order to check the floor plan with the actual pieces. This frequently gives a clearer visualization of the set to be created and contributes to accuracy in the building of new pieces.

10. Make a sketch of each piece that is to be built. From this sketch it is possible to figure exactly how much lumber is necessary

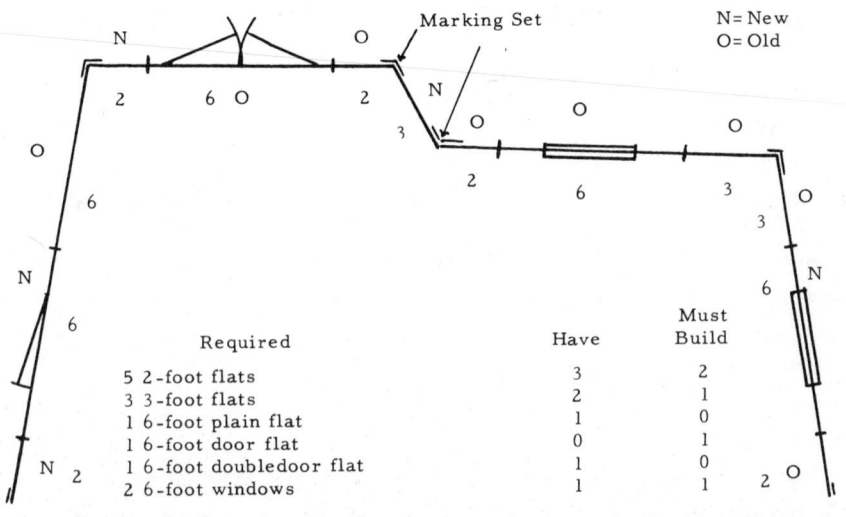

Required	Have	Must Build
5 2-foot flats	3	2
3 3-foot flats	2	1
1 6-foot plain flat	1	0
1 6-foot door flat	0	1
1 6-foot doubledoor flat	1	0
2 6-foot windows	1	1

Fig. 12.—Set Plan, Showing Separate Pieces Required and Set Marking

to build the new set and to estimate the most economical length of lumber to purchase. (See Figure 13.)

11. Give careful consideration to the moving of scenery, particularly if it is necessary to make changes between acts. This should be done before, not after, the sets are built in order to avoid building scenery that cannot be changed readily.

All of the above steps must be taken in consultation with and checked by the director of the play. It is his cast that must use the set, and the set must fit his directing needs to the greatest possible degree, be it proscenium, arena, open, or thrust theatre stage.

SUGGESTIONS FOR SCENE CHANGING

As has been stated above, changes of scenes must be considered at the time of designing and not left to chance after the sets are completed. When changes are to be made, ability to make them rapidly is of prime importance.

Battening Scenery

There are a number of common means by which scene changing is facilitated. Where a loft for flying scenery is available, large sections of wall, including doors, windows, pictures, etc., are arranged

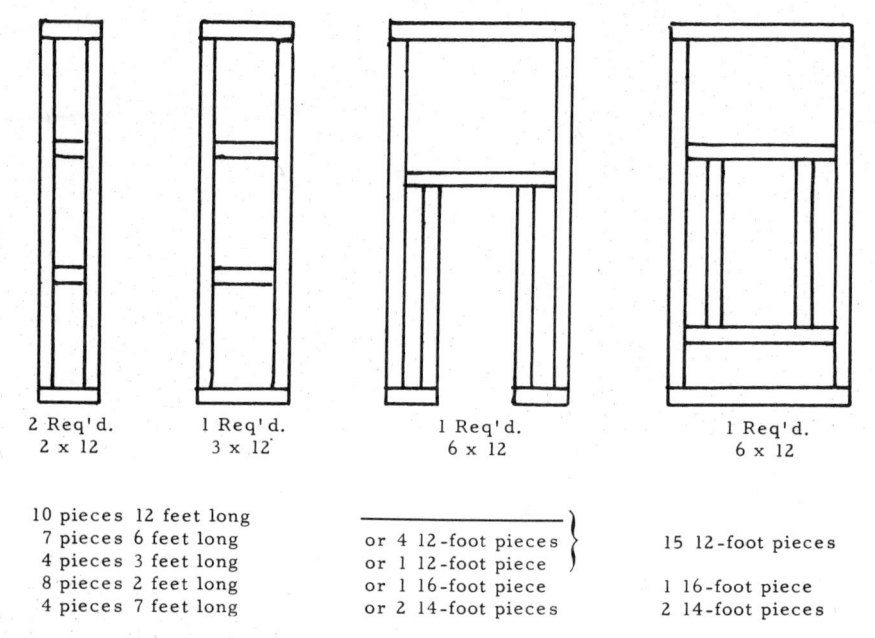

2 Req'd.	1 Req'd.	1 Req'd.	1 Req'd.
2 x 12	3 x 12	6 x 12	6 x 12

10 pieces 12 feet long			
7 pieces 6 feet long	or 4 12-foot pieces	15 12-foot pieces	
4 pieces 3 feet long	or 1 12-foot piece		
8 pieces 2 feet long	or 1 16-foot piece	1 16-foot piece	
4 pieces 7 feet long	or 2 14-foot pieces	2 14-foot pieces	

FIG. 13.—SKETCH OF PIECES TO BE BUILT, SHOWING MATERIAL SPECIFICATIONS

so that they can be raised out of the way or lowered into place at will. This does not mean that these walls are built in one piece; they are assembled from separate flats and battened together in the back with battens that may be nailed or screwed to the scenery.

A batten, in this instance, is a piece of 1 by 3 inch lumber varying in length, depending on the size of the wall to be fastened together. (See Figure 14.)

After the separate flats have been battened together, hanging irons are bolted to the top of the wall at each side and at the center. A hanging iron is a band of iron approximately 1 foot long drilled with three holes. (See Figure 14.) One end of the iron is bent around a ring. Into this ring the ropes for flying the scenery are tied with a bowline knot. (See Figure 44.) When the three lines of a set are secured, the wall may be raised or lowered from the pin rail.

Walls may be battened together even if they are not flown. Battening facilitates handling by reducing the number of pieces to be handled and makes possible the elimination of cracks between flats. In designing scenery it is advisable to avoid the use of very long flat walls. The frequent use of jogs (narrow flats) makes possible smaller walls that are easier to handle. Jogs also help brace a set and add interest to the set design. (See Figure 12.)

Hinging Scenery

Another commonly used means of facilitating scene changes is

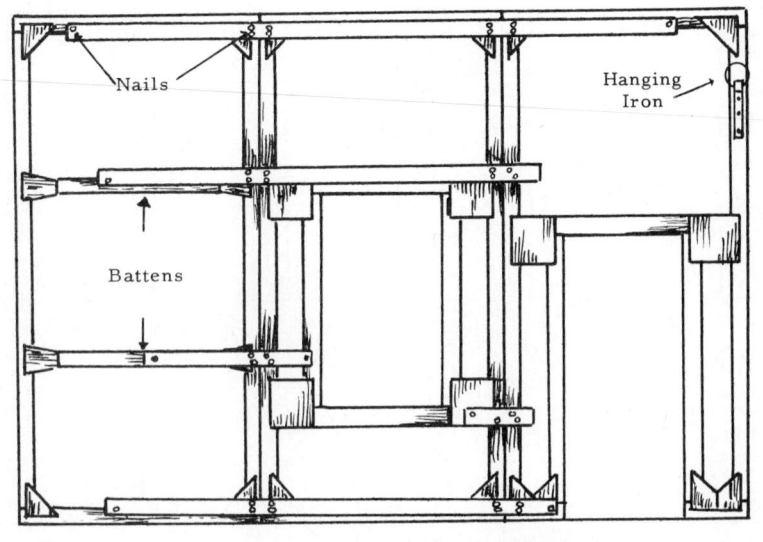

FIG. 14.—SECTIONS OF WALL BATTENED TOGETHER

the hinging together of two or more flats. For example, a side wall of a set may be composed of three flats. If these flats are left as three separate units, each piece must be handled separately when a scene change is made, and time is lost in lashing and unlashing each piece. By hinging the flats together, they can be handled as one unit. A set composed of a great number of small pieces can be reduced to a few large sections. Hinging also makes it possible to fold the flats together so that they require a smaller storage space.

The hinging is accomplished with 2-inch tight-pin backflap hinges, as shown in Figure 15. Usually four are used—one 6 inches from the bottom and one 6 inches from the top, the other two equidistant between. In some instances if there are more than two flats to be hinged a spreader, or knuckle, may be required. This is a 1 by 3 inch piece of lumber hinged between two of the flats. (See Figure 15. For a method of covering the crack and the hinges see Chapter 8.)

Platforms or Wagons

A third method for rapid scenery changes involves the building of low platforms, or wagons, about 6 inches high, varying in size according to where they are to be used. The platforms are mounted on casters. Portions of the set may be assembled on the platforms and rolled into place when needed or pushed to the back of the stage when another set is required. As with other means of facilitating

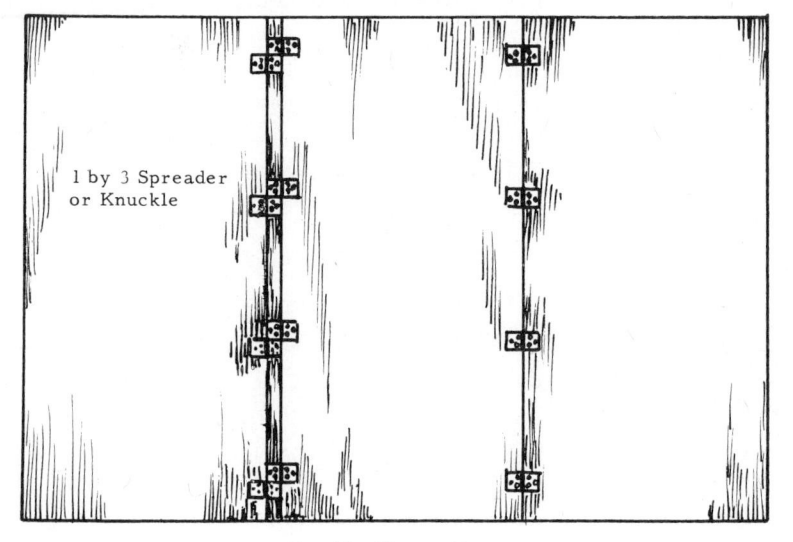

FIG. 15.—HINGED FLATS

scenery changes, platforms must be planned with, and as a part of, the setting itself.

Next in importance to the careful planning of the sets and the way they are to work is the organization of the stage for the production. It is very important to have the handling of all scenes planned and rehearsed carefully before the first performance. This is usually done jointly by the designer, the construction crew, the stage manager, and the stage crew.

Marking the Stage

After the first setting is completed and carefully checked, the floor is marked to show the location of each piece of scenery. This makes for accuracy and speed in re-setting. The marking may be done with chalk (which rubs off easily) or with scene paint (which may be wiped off after the show). (See Figure 12.)

The process of setting and marking is repeated for each set. At the same time, definite locations are assigned to all scenery and furniture used or waiting to be used. A plan is made not only for the particular set in use but also for all the rest of the scenery and properties for the show.

SETTING FOR THE PERFORMANCE

Before each performance the stage should be swept by the prop crew, and all the scenery, properties, and lights checked to make sure that they are in their proper places. One misplaced piece can delay an entire scene change.

When everything is checked, the first set is set. It is then checked by the stage manager. At the given time he will call "places" for the cast. When the cast is assembled, the stage manager gives the electrician the cue to bring up the stage lights and take down the house lights. He then gives the signal to the man on the curtain to open the curtain.

At the end of an act, the stage manager usually gives the cue for closing the curtain, but in some instances the man on the curtain may take his cue directly from the stage. When the curtain is down, the stage manager gives the word for the cast to clear and the stage crew to strike and re-set. Then he repeats the routine of checking sets, calling the cast, etc.

When the play is over, the stage manager has the set struck and the stage cleared, ready for the next night. If it is the last night of the run, the sets are usually disassembled, Dutchmen, battens, and hinges removed, and the separate units made ready for storing until they are reassembled for a new show.

SCENERY FASTENING DEVICES

Setting scenery makes use of a number of devices special to the stage. The most common of these devices are stage braces, jacks, and stage screws, or pegs. Nails are sometimes used instead of stage screws to fasten jacks and braces to the floor. In order to facilitate fastening of scenery to the floor, the flooring of the stage must always be soft wood. The best wood for this purpose is edge-grain fir. Braces may be nailed or screwed to soft wood very easily, with little damage to the floor. This is not true, however, if the stage floor is a polished, hardwood surface. It is impossible to overemphasize the importance of a soft wood floor for a stage.

Stage Braces, Screws, and Jacks

A stage brace is made of two pieces of hardwood about 1¼ inches square, varying in length from 2 to 8 feet. These pieces of wood are bound together at each end with metal bands. In one of the metal bands is a thumb screw, by which it is possible to adjust the length of the brace. At one end of the brace is attached a curved metal strip containing several holes; at the other end is a double hook. The hook is placed into the stage brace cleat on the flat; the other end is screwed to the floor by a stage screw, or peg. Most flats have one brace cleat; additional brace cleats may be added to the flat at

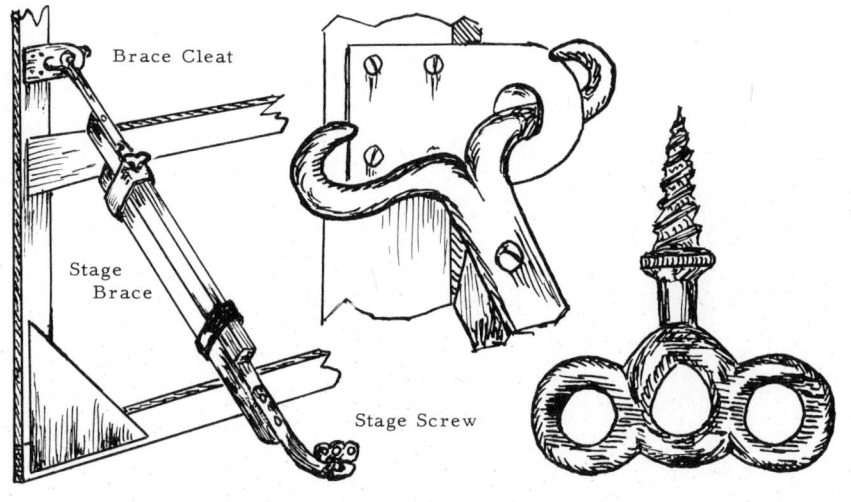

Brace Cleat

Stage Brace

Stage Screw

FIG. 16.—STAGE BRACE, BRACE CLEAT, AND STAGE SCREW

each side of the door opening. These braces keep the set and the door erect and rigid. Sometimes stage screws are used as substitutes for brace cleats. (See Figure 16.)

Frequently a door must be set into a cyc without a flat to hold the door in place. In that case the door is braced in the following manner: Two stage screws are turned into the casing and one into the jamb at the rear of the door. These screws are placed about 5 feet from the floor. Two stage braces are set almost straight back from the casing to keep the door erect. The third brace, attached to the jamb, runs out to the side to keep the door frame square, as shown in Figure 17.

As mentioned above, doors and flats may be held by a jack. A jack is constructed of three pieces of 1 by 3 inch lumber held together by triangles. (See Figure 18.) At the outside point of the right-angle triangle, a strip of metal is attached to the jack. In the metal are three screw holes to hold the strip to the jack and one hole to accommodate a stage screw. A jack is attached to a flat or a door with loose-pin or tight-pin backflap hinges and to the floor with a stage screw.

Lashings

Not only must sets be braced, but, as noted above, the pieces must be lashed together. This is done in the following manner: Two flats are set edge to edge, parallel or at an angle to each other. The lash line is thrown around the top lash cleat and hooked back and

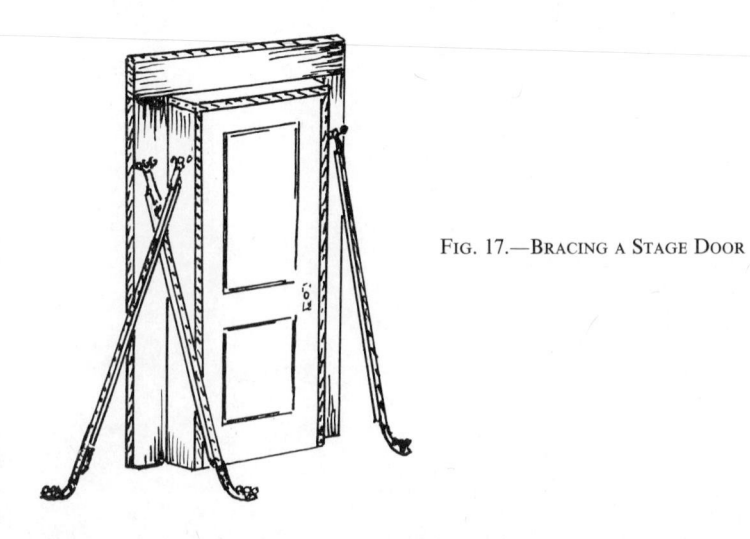

FIG. 17.—BRACING A STAGE DOOR

forth from cleat to cleat until it is tied off on the two cleats at the bottom. (See Figure 19.)

Stage Directions

In order to facilitate backstage operations of both the actors and the stage crew it is necessary to have uniform terminology. Uniformity of terminology in giving directions helps to avoid misunderstanding in the highly complicated operation of presenting a play. Figure 20 shows the divisions of the stage upon which stage direction are based.

First, all directions of right and left are given from the stage facing the audience, not from the audience facing the stage.

Second, toward the footlights is downstage; away from the footlights is upstage. Locations away from the center toward left or right are known as off stage. All directions from the sides to the center are on stage. For example, a chair facing the footlights is facing downstage. If it is turned to face the back wall, it is facing upstage. A piece of scenery that is set at right angles to the footlights is set up and down stage. A chair facing away from the center is facing off stage; turned toward the center it is facing on stage. Scenery parallel to the footlights is set off and on stage. Off stage and on stage may have another meaning. Off stage may mean the space outside of the set, on stage inside the set. Furniture or scenery that is set at an angle to any of the four given directions is said to rake;

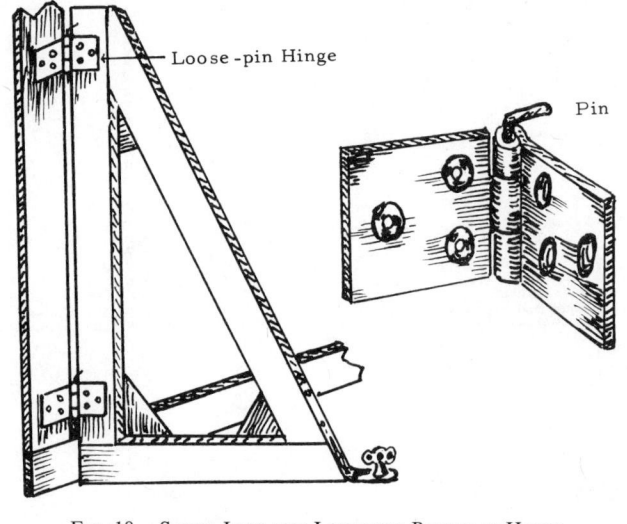

Loose-pin Hinge

Pin

Fig. 18.—Stage Jack and Loose-pin Backflap Hinge

that is, have a position that is neither parallel nor at right angles to the footlights.

Third, all space at the right or left of the stage not occupied by the set is called the wings. All space above the set is called the fly loft, loft, or flies.

Fourth, the distance from the curtain line to the back of the set is called the depth of the set. In some instances, the depth of a set is measured by the location of the border lights—the rows of lights above the stage running parallel to the footlights. The area from the curtain line, or first border light, to the second border light is called "in one"; from the second to the third border light is "in two," and so on until the last border light is passed. The distance beyond that is called full stage.

Fifth, the acting area on the stage is divided into nine parts: up left (usually written U.L.), left center (L.C.), down left (D.L.), up center (U.C.), center (C.), down center (D.C.), up right (U.R.), right center (R.C.), and down right (D.R.).

THE STAGE CREW

The backstage staff is composed of the designer of the set, the technical director, the building and painting crew, the stage manager, and the stage crew that handles the scenery during the performance. Obviously, smooth operation demands careful organization of the backstage workers.

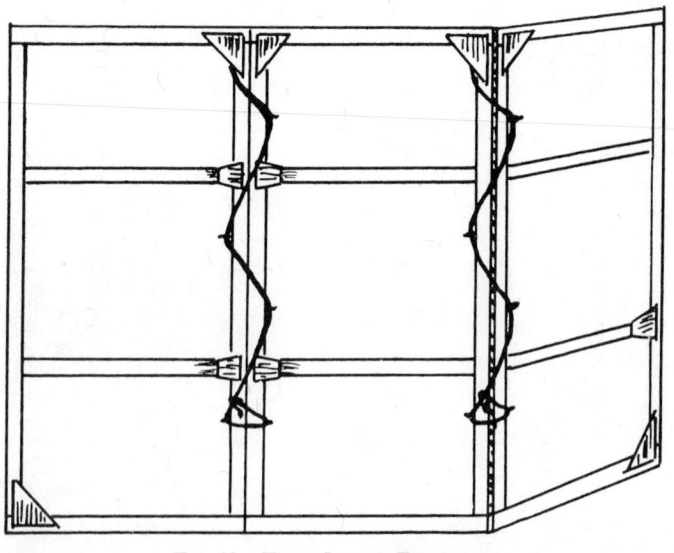

FIG. 19.—FLATS LASHED TOGETHER

In some instances, the designer, builders, stage manager, and stage crew are all the same people, but many times they are not. In any case, the procedure in backstage operation is the same. Since the designer and the builders know how the set goes together they may explain it to or help the stage crew at the first setting. (There are two other crews that are part of the backstage operation, but they are not directly concerned with scenery, properties, and lighting. They are the make-up and costume departments.)

The designer, technical director, and construction crew are responsible for making the scenery. The stage manager and stage crew are responsible for handling the sets and for operation of the stage. In addition, the stage manager is in complete command of activities backstage during a performance. All orders come from him.

Stage Manager

The stage manager is the director's backstage representative during the run of the play. Since his duties are numerous he often has one or more assistants. The stage manager holds book, checks to see that the cast is in the dressing rooms in time for costume changes and make-up, calls time before curtains, checks to see that scenery, properties, and lighting are in order, calls places to the cast, gives curtain and light cues, gives all light and sound cues during the performance, and usually gives curtain cues for the ends of acts. The assistant stage managers do the leg work. The stage manager should be on stage, available at all times. Next to the director, no one knows as much about running the production as the stage manager.

Stage Crew

Although one organization, the stage crew is divided into three

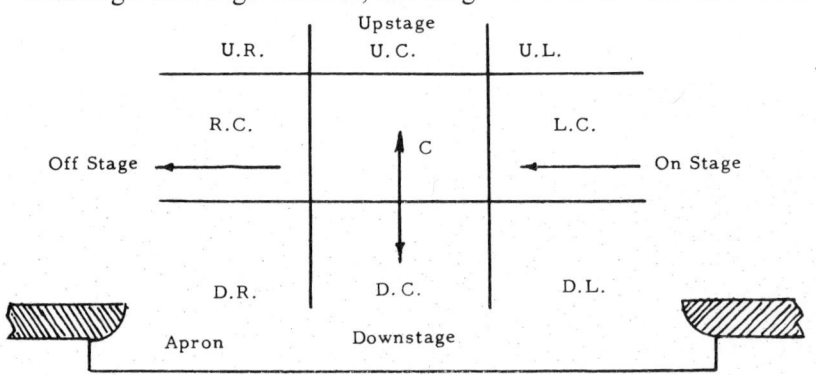

FIG. 20.—STAGE DIRECTIONS

departments: carpentry, electrical, and property. The carpentry department, of which the scenic artists are usually a part in nonprofessional theatres, builds and paints the scenery. The property department borrows, rents, buys, or makes all necessary props. The electrical department arranges all electrical equipment and sees that it is in order.

The master carpenter.—All scenery on the floor and in the flies is handled by the master carpenter and his crew. During performances, the carpenter gives instructions and supervises the work of the crew. If a show is complicated the carpenter supervises one half of the stage and his assistant supervises the other half. People who handle the scenery are called grips. Under the master carpenter is the head flyman, who is in charge of the pin rail or lock rail. He is assisted by flymen. The person who operates the curtain is also in the carpentry department.

The master property man.—All properties are supervised by the master property man. Like the master carpenter, he may have an assistant. The crew that works for the master property man are called props. They are in charge of all furniture, draperies, pictures, dishes, rugs, food, hand-operated sound effects, general set dressing, all objects handled by the actors (such as cigars, cigarettes, lighters, handkerchiefs, fans), and all such miscellany. In addition, props are the housekeepers of the stage. They sweep both on the stage and off, vacuum, dust, and wash dishes. Off-stage sweeping is particularly essential under all conditions. It should be done before every performance.

The master electrician.—The master electrician is in charge of all lighting. The members of his crew are called operators. If a follow spotlight is used from out in the auditorium, the person who operates that light is the front light operator. In conjunction with the director or scene designer, the master electrician supervises the setting of all lights, including practical floor lamps, table lamps, wall brackets, and orchestra racks, if necessary. The work, however, is done by the operators, who also operate electrical sound effects. The master electrician usually runs the switchboard.

It is impossible to overemphasize the importance of a high degree of co-operation and co-ordination between all departments on the stage. Department heads should map every move with great care and then give detailed instructions to their crews. Nothing should be left to chance. Such care and instruction will insure the orderly movement of all parts of the operation. A crew should be as carefully rehearsed as the cast of the play. Although the stage crew is not seen, it is equally important to a smooth, successful production.

PRODUCTION SCHEDULE

It is impossible to establish criteria for the production schedule for all plays, because no two plays present the same problems and no two productions are the same. There may even be variation from production to production in the same theatre. In general, therefore, the following points should be kept in mind in establishing the production schedule for a particular play.

1. The floor plans and sketches should be approved by the director about the time that he starts to rehearse the play, because they are essential to his operation.

2. The general construction and assembly of flats should be completed about three weeks before production.

3. The set should be coated-in ready for decorating about two weeks in advance of the performance.

4. The major portion of the work should be completed the week before the show. This will give time for final adjustments and emergencies.

5. The crews should have two or three rehearsals with the scenery prior to dress rehearsal, which should be in all respects exactly like a performance. Do not believe that "tomorrow night it will be all right." Tomorrow night is too late.

6. Substitute properties are frequently needed at rehearsal almost immediately.

7. All regular props should be available for rehearsal about three days in advance of production dates. It is true that some perishable props cannot be provided this soon, but actors must become accustomed to handling everything that they are going to use during performances.

8. Although electricians cannot start to work until a set is in place, all electrical equipment should be ready so that it can be set as soon as the scenery is available.

9. Again, the electricians should have at least three rehearsals.

10. In their interest in actors and in the play, directors frequently forget that the stage crew needs time to work. Definite times should be made available for this purpose, and they should not be times that no one else would want to work, such as meal times, midnight, and Sunday mornings. The members of the stage crew are human, too.

3

CYCLORAMAS

TYPES OF SETS

Stage settings can be divided into three types as follows: wings and backdrop, cyclorama, or cyc, and box set. Combinations of these three types of sets are possible. Set pieces may also be added.

Wings and Backdrop Sets

The oldest of the three types of sets is the wings and backdrop type, and it is perhaps the least used now, except for special cases where painted realism or stylization is required by the play. A wing is two pieces of scenery hinged together so that they stand at an angle. There are usually two or more of these pieces at each side of the stage, the number depending on the depth of the set. Back of these sets of wings a drop is hung. A drop is a large piece of cloth, the size depending upon the size of the stage, painted to match the wings. Wings are frequently painted to represent trees (wood wings), and the backdrop to represent forest and sky. Wings and backdrop may, however, represent anything from a marble palace (palace wings) to abstract space.

Cyc Sets

A cyclorama, or cyc, has come to mean any kind of material that is hung on battens in such a manner that it encloses the acting area. Strictly speaking, however, a cyc is a plaster dome in the shape of a quarter of a sphere which, when lighted, gives the effect of sky. With the borrowing of the term for other purposes, this type of cyc is now usually called a sky dome or horizant. Consequently, there are as many kinds of cycs as there are kinds of material: blue sky cycs, gray rep cycs, black velour cycs, etc. The word cyc refers to the way in which the material is hung, not to what it is made of, what it looks like, or the use to which it is put.

Box Sets

A box set is made from flats. A flat is a wood frame covered with cloth and painted. (See Chapter 4 for discussion of flats.) The box set starts at the tormentor or return and runs upstage, across the back, and down the other side, completely enclosing the playing space. Box sets usually represent some type of room.

Set Pieces

The term "set pieces" covers a variety of special kinds of scenery, such as rocks, stumps, walls, houses, and ground rows. A ground row is a specialized form of set piece located in front of a backdrop or cyc, usually with space between the two for lighting. A ground row may be a realistic wall, a distant hill or landscape, or it may be an abstraction.

BORDERS AND CEILINGS

Each of the three types of sets described above requires some device to prevent the audience from seeing the open space above the set. This is accomplished in three ways: As with cycloramas, the scenery may be built high so that it is impossible to see above it. Borders may be constructed to mask the top of the scenery. Or, thirdly, a ceiling may be used.

Borders

Borders are pieces of scenery similar to a teaser. Borders are usually made to match the rest of the set and are hung from side to side of the stage. They hang far enough down into the set to cover or mask the upper edge of the scenery. The number of borders used varies with the size of the set. For exteriors, blue sky borders or foliage borders may be used. A cyclorama uses borders of the same material as the cyc itself. Borders may also be used in a box set, though a ceiling is preferable.

Ceilings

A ceiling is a single piece of cloth on a frame large enough to cover the top of the set. It is painted either a light color, as most ceilings in rooms are, or the same color as the particular set with which it is used. The ceiling is raised on two sets of lines; it is lowered to rest on top of the set after the set is in place. (For the construction of ceilings see Chapter 4.)

MAKING CYCLORAMAS

Two of the many types of cycloramas commonly used are the painted cyc and the unpainted cyc. They differ in construction as described below.

Painted Cycs

An example of the painted cyc is the sky cyc, which is to be painted blue. The painted cyc is made of the widest unbleached muslin obtainable in order to reduce the number of seams in the cyc. The seams must run horizontally. If they run vertically, painting may cause the cloth to shrink unevenly.

The top of the cyc should be finished with webbing, which is heavy cotton or hemp tape about 3 inches wide. Into this webbing, grommets are set. Grommets are heavy brass eyelets. They are usually obtainable from a tent and awning company. They are set into the webbing 12 to 18 inches apart, as shown in Figure 21.

The bottom of the sky cyc may be finished like the top with webbing, or it may be finished with a 4-inch hem or pocket. The first method is perhaps better, since the use of grommets makes it easy to tie the cyc to the floor. A tie line should be fastened to each grommet. The tie lines may be mason line or Venetian-blind cord. Equally good and much cheaper is the cotton tape used by tent and awning companies for binding canvas.

Borders that are to be painted to match a cyc should be made in the same way, except that no webbing or pocket is needed in the

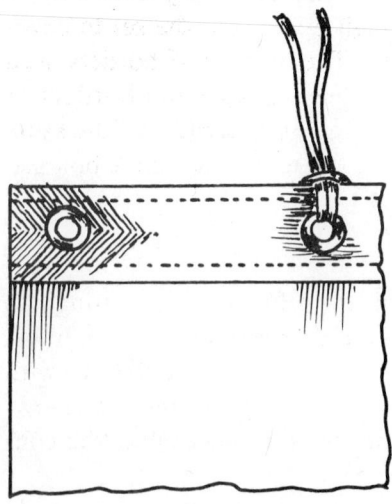

FIG. 21.—WEBBING AND GROMMETS FOR CYCS

bottom of a border. Not even a hem is necessary. A border should have at least a 6-foot drop.

A painted backdrop is also made in the same way. In fact, this same method of construction may be applied to all hanging scenery that is to be painted.

Unpainted Cycs

An unpainted cyc is made with seams running vertically. The top is finished with webbing. The pocket or hem at the bottom of the unpainted cyc is made to hold a light chain, which is particularly necessary if the cyc is made of light material. If a heavy velour is used, a chain is not essential. When a chain is used it is advisable to line the pocket with unbleached muslin in order to prevent the chain from wearing through the bottom of the cyc. The chain should be sewed to the pocket at intervals to keep it from sliding.

Materials for Cycs

Cycs for general use are most commonly made of duvetyn, sateen, rep, and velour. They range in price in that order—duvetyn is the cheapest and velour the most expensive. The most serviceable colors are gray, tan, and black. A light blue cyc is very valuable, but it is used primarily as a sky and therefore does not have the variety of uses other colors have.

In order to provide fullness for certain types of cycloramas, fullness is sometimes built in with a series of inverted pleats along the top. This is not advisable. The fullness should be adjusted as the cyc is hung, not sewed in permanently. From one-third to one-half of the material is allowed for the fullness required.

If the cyc is to be made of velour, care should be taken to have the nap run in one direction. Borders may be made in two ways. If the material to be used has a definite nap or pattern, the seam should run up and down. If there is no nap or pattern, the material should run the long way of the border parallel to the floor.

USING CYCLORAMAS

A cyc to be used for a wide variety of purposes should be made in a number of pieces, not less than six, preferably more. Nine or ten pieces of varying widths would not be too many. A variety of pieces makes it possible to have a variety of locations for openings. In addition to the long sections of the cyc there should be a number of short pieces approximately 6½ feet shorter than the cyc and 6 to 9 feet wide. Hung into the set at intervals with the rest of the cyc they form openings for doors and windows. There should be also two or three pieces about 3 feet long to fill in the spaces beneath windows. (See Figure 22.)

Height of a Cyc

The height of a cyc is based almost entirely upon the height of the stage. If the stage is very low, the cyclorama should extend to the ceiling. On a stage with a loft the height of the cyc may be determined by the height of the loft. The cyclorama should be constructed so that it may be raised to permit working and setting scenery beneath it. The average height of a cyclorama is 16 to 24 feet.

Cyc Battens

A set of battens for a cyc may be made of pipe or wood. The battens consist of three pieces: one for the back, which is hung on a set of lines, and the other two for the arms, one on each side. If the battens are made of pipe, the arms are held to the back batten by a pipe knuckle, which may be purchased from a stage hardware company. If the battens are made of wood, the arms are held in place by 6-inch strap hinges. The downstage ends of the arms are held by the long and short lines of a set of lines or by special lines called trips.

A small sand bag should be permanently attached to the trip line about 3 feet above the ends. Harness or rope snaps should be attached to the ends. On the downstage ends of the cyc arms, about

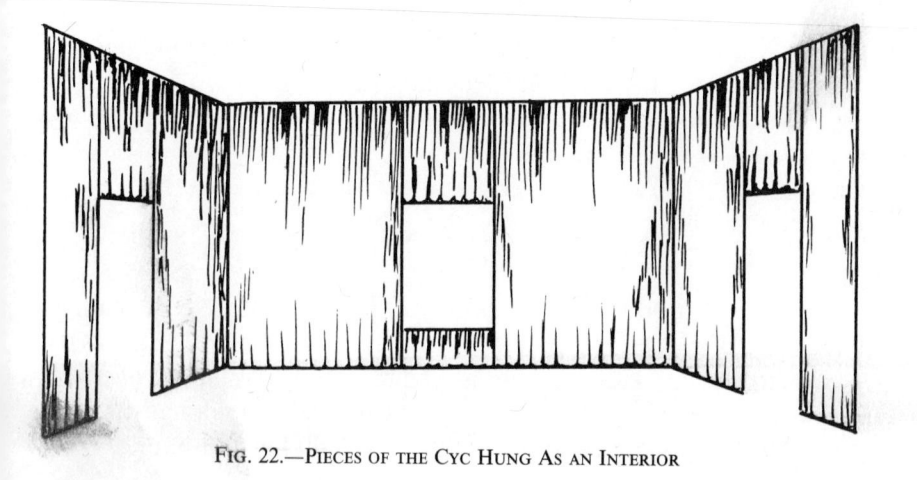

FIG. 22.—PIECES OF THE CYC HUNG AS AN INTERIOR

6 feet of sash cord should be tied. A loop is made in the free end of this line, and when the arms are to be raised the snaps of the trip lines are snapped into the loops, enabling the arm to be fastened and unfastened with great rapidity. (See Figure 23.)

Round Cyc

Occasionally a cyc is hung from a curved pipe to give the effect of being round. Such a batten is difficult to handle and is hard to trim. (A cyc is in trim when it rests evenly on the floor and has no undesirable wrinkles.) The same general effect of roundness may be obtained with less difficulty by adding two diagonals to the ordinary battens. These two diagonals are attached to the back batten about three-quarters of the distance from the center line to the side arm and then to the side arms. The diagonals cut off the two corners of the cyc and make a five-sided batten and a five-sided cyc, as shown in Figure 24. When hung, this cyc has the appearance of being almost round.

Cyc Attached to the Ceiling

If there are no facilities for hanging a cyc on lines, five large screw eyes may be screwed into the ceiling, one at each of the two down-stage corners and three across the back of the stage. Five large harness or rope snaps may be attached to the batten, and the cyc can then be snapped up or taken down with very little difficulty. If the reason pulleys and sheaves are not allowed is that they are unsightly, screw eyes should prove satisfactory, since they are very inconspicuous.

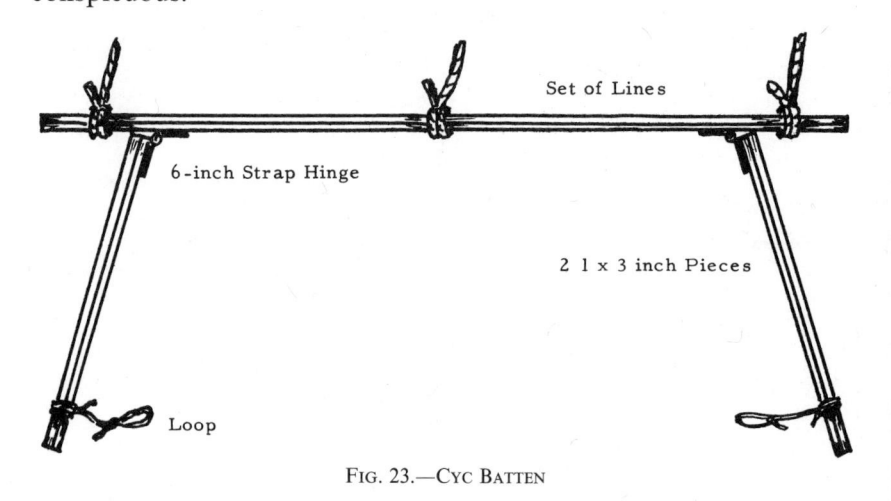

Set of Lines

6-inch Strap Hinge

2 1 x 3 inch Pieces

Loop

FIG. 23.—CYC BATTEN

Tying on the Cyc

Pieces of a cyc tied to a batten should overlap about 18 inches, and it is important that the pieces to be attached to the arms be lapped properly. Tying from front to back, the downstage end of the second piece should tie behind the upstage end of the first piece. If the cyc is to be draped, each section should be tied in the following manner: Ascertain where each piece is to start and tie both ends. Then tie the center tie-line of the piece halfway between the two ends. Next tie on the two centers of each side made by centering the piece, and so on until all ties are tied. (See Figure 25.) In this way the drape in the cyc will be evenly distributed. If the cyc is to be tied on without any drape, start either at the center and tie out toward the ends or start at one downstage corner and tie around to the other side.

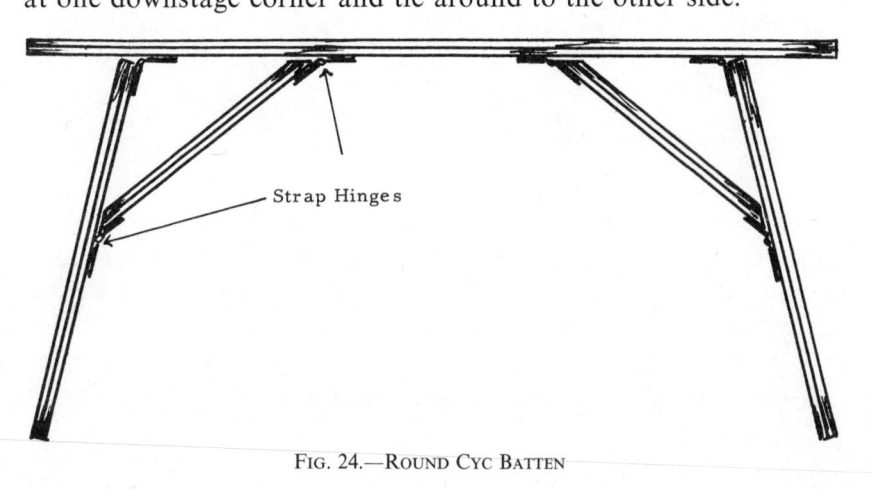

Strap Hinges

FIG. 24.—ROUND CYC BATTEN

FIG. 25.—TYING ON THE CYC

VARIATIONS IN THE USE OF CYCS

Contrary to the rather widely held opinion that a cyc solves all scenic problems, a cyc is as limited in its use as any other type of scenery, and it should not be used constantly for all kinds of sets and for all types of shows. If a cyc must be used extensively every possible effort should be made to vary its appearance by changing its size, shape, and arrangement from show to show. The possibilities of changing the appearance of a cyc are limited only by the ingenuity of the stage craftsman.

Legs

One variation is the use of the pieces of the cyc as legs and backdrop. This is a slight variation on the arrangement of wings and backdrop discussed at the beginning of this chapter. Part of the cyc material is used as a backdrop. The rest is hung in pairs of panels on each side of the stage. These hanging legs take the place of wings. The number of panels, or legs, depends on how large the set is to be. (See Figure 26.)

Vignette

Another use for a cyc is as a background for a vignette, or cut-down set, which is a variation on a box set. A vignette is made of flats set inside a cyc. These flats are usually 8 to 10 feet high and

FIG. 26.—LEGS AND BACKDROP FROM PIECES OF CYC

are arranged to form a simple box set. The upper edge of the set may be plain, or it may have a profiled upper edge. This type of set may be realistic, decorative, or abstract. (See Figure 27.)

FIG. 27.—VIGNETTE

4

FLATS AND SET PIECES

Box sets are made up of flats and jogs of various styles and widths according to the requirements of the play. There are three types of standard flats but as many special styles as there are designs for settings. The three standard flats are (1) plain flats, (2) door flats, and (3) window flats. A door flat is built with an opening into which a door casing may be placed. A window flat is built with an opening into which a window casing may be set. With these exceptions, door flats and window flats are the same as plain flats. (See Figure 28.)

Flats may vary in width, but they usually do not exceed 5 feet 9 inches. The height varies according to the design of the set or according to the stage on which the flats are to be used. If the height of the stage permits, flats should be at least 12 feet high; certainly no less. The average height of flats may be 12, 14, or 16 feet. Some scenery may be as much as 24 feet or more in height.

For adaptation to small stages, flats frequently are as narrow as 5 feet. The most satisfactory width, however, is 6 feet, rather than the standard 5 feet 9 inches noted above. The 5 feet 9 inch width came to be taken as standard as a result of a necessity which had no direct connection with the stage. When dramatic productions were taken on the road, it was necessary to ship scenery as baggage. The doors to baggage cars were so small that scenery wider than 5 feet 9 inches could not be put into the cars. Baggage car doors are now made large enough to take scenery of almost any size, and, furthermore, amateurs are seldom faced with the problem of shipping scenery. The advantage of 6-foot scenery is obvious. Measurements are simplified, and material can be cut to better advantage with less waste.

Jogs are similar to flats, except that they are usually half the width of a standard flat. Jogs may be as narrow as 1 foot or as wide as 4 feet. All flats less than 4 feet wide are classed as jogs. It is possible to have door or window openings in jogs, but they are not common. Regardless of width, flats and jogs are built on the same principle.

TOOLS AND MATERIALS

Tools for Building Flats

Tools for building flats are the same as those for most forms of simple carpentry: hammers—preferably a ripping hammer and a tack hammer (a staple gun may be used in place of the hammers) —a standard crosscut saw, an 18-inch or 24-inch steel square, screw drivers, and a clinching iron, which is a piece of flat boilerplate iron approximately ¼ inch thick and 1 foot square. The clinching iron may be obtained from a foundry or a salvage yard. For building scenery it may be advisable to have a more elaborate set of tools, including brace and bit, chisels, hack saws, C-clamps, etc., but they are not necessary for building flats. Power tools, if available, are great time-savers and labor-savers. The most useful are table saw, band saw, drill press, and turning lathe.

Lumber for Scenery

The lumber most commonly used for constructing scenery is ordinary white pine. The standard size used for building flats is 1 by 3—

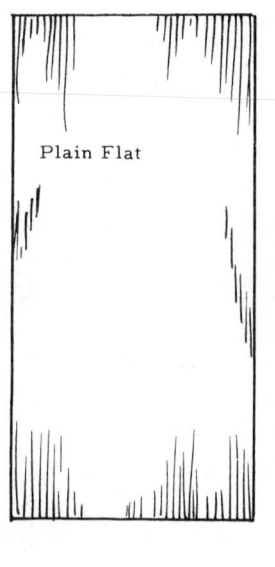
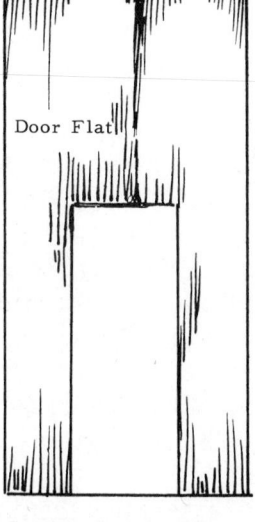
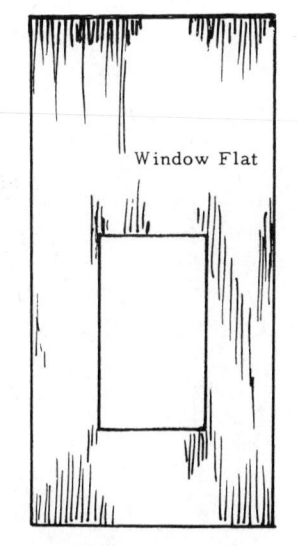

Plain Flat   Door Flat   Window Flat

FIG. 28.—STANDARD FLATS

that is, 1 inch thick by 3 inches wide. The length of the lumber will of course depend on the requirements of advantageous cutting. Lumber comes in lengths of 12, 14, and 16 feet.

It should be noted here that standard, or stock, sizes of lumber are quite different from the sizes specified when ordering. Lumber is cut to full sizes, but when it is dressed, or planed, to make it smooth, it is about ¼ inch under full measurement. For example, 1 by 3 inch lumber actually measures ¾ by 2¾ inches. This fact should be remembered when ordering lumber. If exact dimensions are required, they should be specified when ordering. Then the lumber will be cut from wider boards, and the cost will be increased accordingly. When lumber sizes are mentioned here, it should be understood that standard, or stock, sizes are meant. For example, 1 by 3 means ¾ by 2¾.

One other fact should be remembered when ordering lumber. Lumber is usually sold in board feet. A board foot is 1 foot long, 1 foot wide, and 1 inch thick. For example, if 100 feet of 1 by 3 inch lumber is required to build a certain amount of scenery, it will amount to exactly 25 board feet, since four boards 3 inches wide can be cut from a piece of lumber 1 foot wide. Therefore, in ordering 100 feet of 1 by 3 inch lumber it is wise to specify linear feet. Then the lumber company cannot misinterpret the order and deliver 100 board feet—400 linear feet of lumber. Ordering in linear feet is usually less confusing to those who are not accustomed to buying lumber.

Keystones and Corners

Keystones and corners are necessary in building flats. They are made of three-ply veneer—plywood—¼ inch thick. Almost any kind of wood facing on the plywood will do. Fir plywood is usually the cheapest, but it is by no means the best. Birch plywood is unquestionably the strongest.

Keystones and corners may be ordered made up at almost any lumber company or may be made up in the theatre workshop. They also may be ordered ready-made from any stage hardware company.

A keystone is a piece of ¼ inch three-ply veneer 8 inches long, 4 inches wide on one end, and 3 inches wide at the other end. (See Figure 29.) This piece therefore is in the shape of the keystone used in the center of a stone arch. The outside grain of the wood must run the length of the keystone.

A corner, or triangle, is a piece of three-ply veneer ¼ inch thick cut in the shape of a right triangle 10 inches long on the two right angle sides. (See Figure 29.)

Hardware

The hardware needed for building flats is: 1¼-inch iron clout nails, threepenny fine blued lath nails, staples, 4-ounce tacks, and sash cord or braided cotton clothesline. If economy is necessary sixteen-penny spikes or 2-inch roundhead blue screws may be used for lash cleats. If money is readily available special stage hardware, such as lashline eyes, stage brace cleats, and lashline hooks or cleats, may be purchased.

Cloth for Covering Flats

The material used to cover flats is unbleached muslin. Muslin may be purchased in a variety of grades and widths. The very best quality of muslin is not necessary unless a permanent set is being built. On the other hand, poor quality muslin is difficult to paint and wears out rapidly.

Yard-wide muslin is called four-quarter muslin. Other widths are five-quarter, six-quarter, seven-quarter, eight-quarter (two yards wide), nine-quarter, and ten-quarter. It can be seen that it is possible to buy muslin in a width which can be used with the least possible waste.

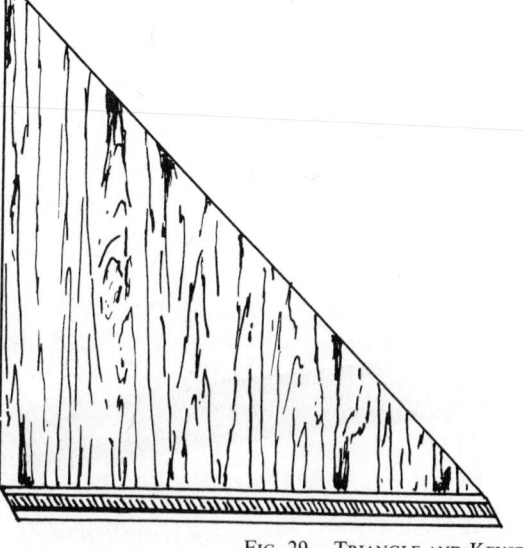
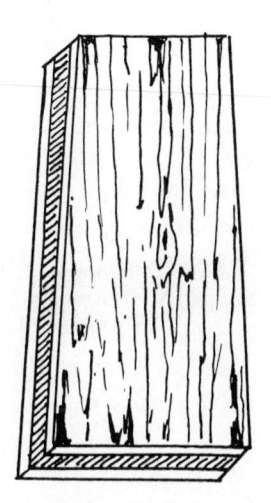

FIG. 29.—TRIANGLE AND KEYSTONE

The Pieces of a Flat

The wood framework of a flat is usually made of six pieces: two side stiles (the long upright pieces that determine the height of the flat), one top and one bottom rail (the pieces that determine the width of the flat), and two center, or toggle, rails, which strengthen the side stiles.

Cutting the Pieces

The side stiles should be 5½ inches shorter than the height of the finished flat. For example, for a 12-foot flat the stiles are cut 11 feet 6½ inches long. Thus, the stiles fit between the rails, and the whole flat is 12 feet high. The top and bottom rails are cut the full width of the flat to form a base on which to slide the flat when it is moved. The two center rails are cut 5½ inches shorter than the width of the flat.

Assembling the Pieces

In assembling the pieces of the flat, the top and bottom rails are placed on the floor and the side stiles placed between them. Then the two center rails are placed so that they divide the flat into three equal spaces, as shown in Figure 30. If only a few flats are to be built, a large steel square may be used to square the corners of the flats. If many flats are to be built, it will be worth while to nail two pieces of 1 by 3 inch lumber to the floor at right angles to form a square in which to build the flats. More elaborate is a special table on which to construct scenery. However, such a table is impractical for most amateurs because of cost, size, and weight.

Applying Keystones and Corners

Next, when the corners of the flat are square, a triangle is placed on each corner with the grain of the triangle parallel to the side stile, or across the joint. The triangle must be set in ¾ inch from both the side and the end of the flat. (See Figure 30.) The triangles are held in place by clout nails, which are driven through the corner and about halfway into the lumber. Although not as good, threepenny fine blued lath nails or staples may be used.

The toggle rails, which are set at right angles to the sides of the flat, are held in place by keystones, as shown in Figure 30. Here, also, keystones must be set in ¾ inch from the edge of the flat. Keystones and corners are set back the thickness of a piece of lumber so that two flats can be set together at right angles and still form a snug joint.

In nailing the keystones and corners in place it is well to get the greatest amount of strength with the smallest number of nails. Ten clout nails are used—five in each of the two pieces of the frame the keystone or corner is holding together—and they are placed like the five spots on a playing card, as shown in Figure 30.

Clinching Clout Nails

When all the keystones and corners have been nailed in place a clinching iron is placed under the corner, and, in turn, the nails are driven in the rest of the way and clinched over against the iron. One and one-fourth inch clout nails are used because the nails must clinch as they go through the lumber. The corners and keystones are ¼ inch thick; the lumber is ¾ inch. Thus, ¼ inch of the nail is left for clinching—an absolute minimum if the keystones and corners are to hold.

Steps in Making Door and Window Flats

Window Flats

A window flat differs from a plain flat in two respects. In a window flat the center rails are set to form the bottom and top of the window opening. The average window is approximately 30 inches from the floor and about as high as a door—6½ feet. Of course, the size of the window may vary with the design of the set. The other difference between the plain flat and the window flat is the addition of two upright stiles set between the rails in the window flat to form the sides of the window opening. The average window width is 30 inches. The stiles forming the window opening are held in place by corners. (See Figure 31.) If the flat is very tall, a third rail may be necessary halfway between the top of the window and the top of the flat.

Door Flats

In building a door flat, one cross rail is set at the top of the door. (The average door is from 6½ to 7 feet high.) Two upright stiles are cut to fit between the rail forming the top of the door and the rail at the bottom of the flat. These pieces form the sides of the door opening. (The average door is 30 inches wide.) The stiles are held in place by corners. After the flat is completed, the portion of the bottom rail between the two side stiles of the door opening is sawed out. (See Figure 32.)

Foot irons.—To strengthen the door flat after the bottom rail has been removed for the door opening, a foot or door iron is screwed to the bottom of the flat. The foot iron may be made in three different styles. It may be a straight piece of iron the width of the flat, with two or three holes at each end. A second style may be a piece of metal approximately 2 feet longer than the width of the flat, turned up at each end to form a U-shape. Holes are drilled in the sides as well as the bottom of the iron. The third style of foot iron is a piece of iron 4 to 6 feet long with two pieces of iron about 1 foot long attached to the inside of the door opening. This style of foot iron is also drilled for screw holes so that it may be screwed to the sides of the door opening and to the bottom of the flat. Although very strong, this type is the least practical of the three types described because it fits only one width of door opening.

Band iron ³⁄₁₆ inch thick and ¾ inch wide is used for making foot irons. Foot irons may be made locally or purchased from a

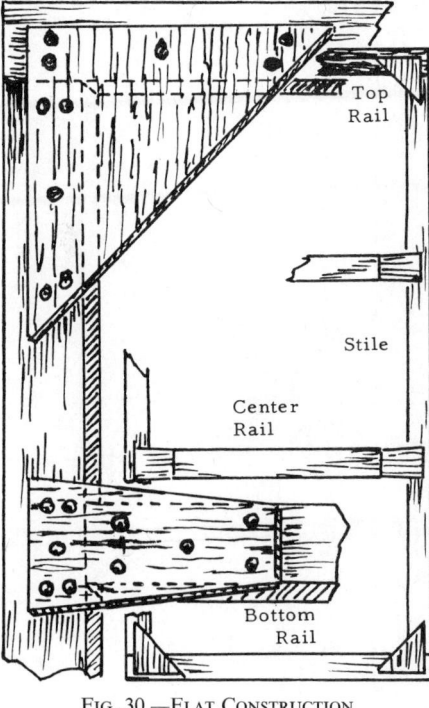

FIG. 30.—FLAT CONSTRUCTION

Top Rail

Stile

Center Rail

Bottom Rail

FIG. 31.—WINDOW FLAT

stage hardware company. If they are made, care should be taken to have all the screw holes countersunk in order to insure a smooth bottom surface.

To allow for the thickness of the foot iron in the height of the door flat, the door flat may be built 3/16 inch shorter than other flats. If the iron runs up the side of the flat, 3/16 inch must be cut out of each side so that the iron will not project beyond the edge of the flat.

LASHING AND CLOTHING FLATS

Lash Cleats

Some form of lash cleats must be added to all flats. Lash cleats may be sixteenpenny spikes, 2-inch blued screws, or professional lashline cleats. The cleats are placed on the back of the flat as shown in Figure 32. The first cleat is placed 18 inches from the top of the upper left-hand corner. The second cleat is placed about 1 foot above

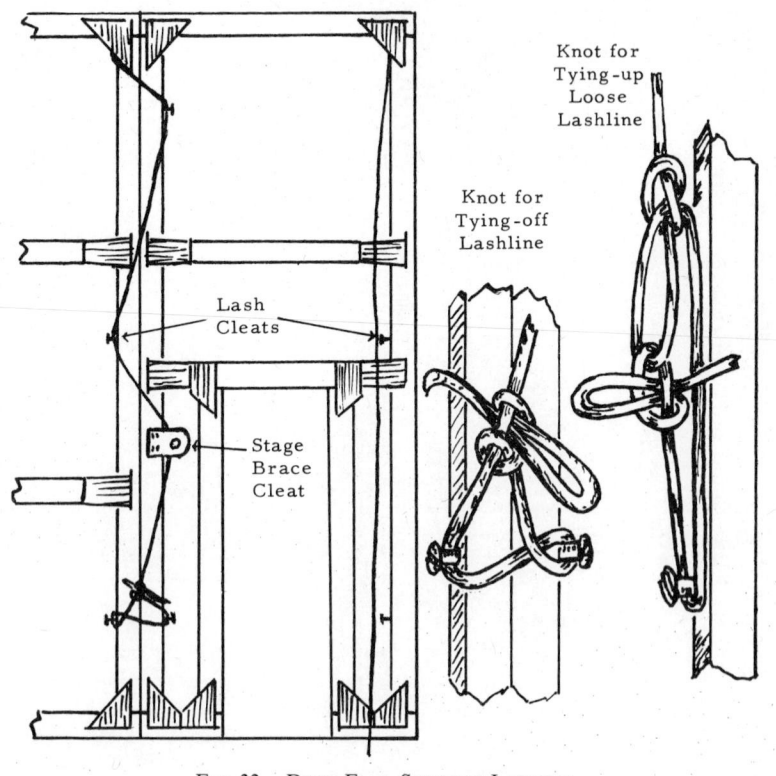

FIG. 32.—DOOR FLAT, SHOWING LASHLINE

the center on the right side of the flat. The third cleat is placed about 1 foot below center on the left side of the flat. The fourth and fifth cleats are placed directly opposite each other on either side of the flat 3 feet from the bottom.

If stage brace cleats are available it is well to substitute one of them for one of the center cleats. A stage brace cleat is a 3 by 6 inch metal plate with a hole at one end, into which a stage brace may be hooked, and four screw holes at the other end for attaching the cleat to the flat. (See Figure 32.)

Lashlines

The lashline (sash cord) is attached to the back of the flat as high up in the upper right corner as possible. There are several methods for attaching the lashline to the flat. A hole may be drilled in the center of the triangle. A knot is tied in the end of the lashline and the line is threaded through the hole and pulled through to the knot. Another method is to place a screw eye in the corner. The line is then knotted and threaded downward through the eye. A regular lashline eye may be purchased for this purpose.

The easiest method of attaching the lashline involves the use of two sixpenny nails. The line is simply nailed securely into the corner. When lines are attached in this manner they are less apt to be removed from the flat. It should be stressed here that a lashline should never be removed from a piece of scenery.

The lashline should be approximately 12 inches longer than the flat. If possible, it should be a single piece of cord without knots or splices. When not in use, the line should be tied up out of the way, as shown in Figure 32.

Clothing the Frame

To clothe the frame, the flat is placed on the floor with keystones and corners down and covered with unbleached muslin. The cloth should be cut to the proper length, not torn. However, if the cloth is too wide, it may be torn to width. The selvage should be torn from both sides before the material is tacked to the frame.

Then the muslin is laid across the frame. Care should be taken to avoid pulling or stretching the material. The cloth is tacked first along the inside edge of one of the side stiles with 4-ounce tacks placed approximately 4 inches apart. Staples—and a stapling gun—may be used in place of tacks and tack hammer. Again, care should be taken to hold the muslin smooth and even.

Next, the cloth is tacked along the inside edge of one of the end rails. Then, with the cloth held even with the outside edge of the other stile, the sides are finished by tacking the muslin to the inside edge of the other side stile. To finish the job, the remaining end is tacked to the inside edge of the last rail. It cannot be emphasized too strongly that the cloth must not be pulled tight when it is tacked to the frame. What is wanted is merely a smooth fit with no slack. (See Figure 33.) If the cloth is pulled tight, warped flats may result.

Door and window flats are covered in the same manner as plain flats. In covering window flats, the outside edges are tacked first. Then tacks are placed around the window opening on the edge away from the opening. After the tacking is completed, the cloth may be removed from the window opening. This same method is used in covering a door flat.

When the tacking is finished, there remains a loose flap of cloth approximately 2 inches wide all around the frame. This flap is glued to the frame as described below.

Gluing the Cloth Edges

After the cloth has been tacked to the frame, all the edges must be glued. There are several preparations that may be used for this purpose, but the cheapest, most satisfactory, and easiest to use is a mixture of 1 pound of dissolved ground sizing glue and 5 pounds of whiting, a white powder that forms the base of most scene paints. A paste is made of this mixture, and it is diluted so that it may be applied evenly and freely with a large brush to the wood under the free edge of the muslin. Experi-

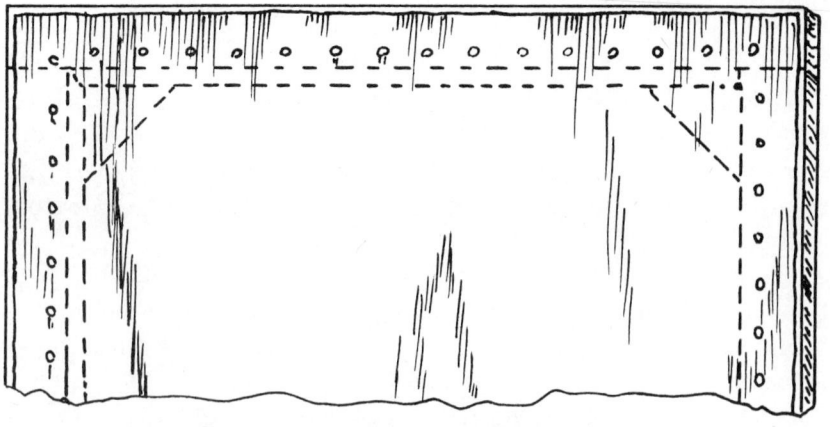

FIG. 33.—TACKING CLOTH ON THE FLAT FRAME

ence is the best guide in getting the mixture to the right consistency. It should never be so thick as to seem sticky or gummy or so thin as to seem watery or sloppy.

After the glue mixture has been applied to the wood under the free edge of the muslin, the cloth is pressed down in place, glue is brushed over the cloth, and the cloth is well soaked to the board.

Care should be taken to avoid running or dropping the glue on the flats. Runs and drops harden and cause trouble later in painting the flat. They do not take paint well, but form large lumps and often appear a different color.

The glue should be allowed to dry before the flat is painted. (See Chapter 8.) If the edges have not been securely glued, or if painting is started before the edges are thoroughly dry, the cloth will pull away from the frame and will have to be re-glued.

ARCHES FOR DOORS AND WINDOWS

Depending upon the set design, doors and windows must sometimes be arched with either a pointed or a rounded top. Arches do not change the major construction of the flat; they merely change the batten which forms the top of the door or window.

Pattern for the Arch

A paper pattern of one-half the arch should be made first. The piece of paper on which the pattern is made should be slightly larger than the height of the arch and half its width. The arch may be drawn free hand or with a compass, depending upon the type of the arch. A second line is then drawn following the curve of the first line. The two lines should be approximately 3 inches apart. (See Figure 34.) The pattern is cut from the paper and placed on a board as described below.

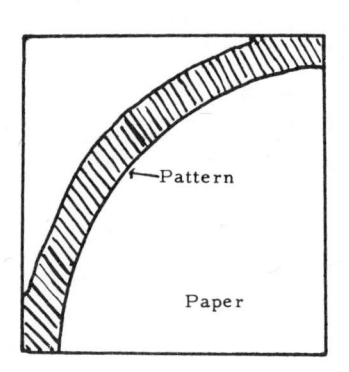

FIG. 34.—PATTERN FOR THE ARCH

Cutting the Arch

The paper pattern is placed on a wide board and traced twice to make the two halves which will form the complete arch. Common white pine is usually used, but the arch may be cut from ¾ inch plywood. If the arch is large, more than one board may be necessary.

A band saw may be used to cut out the arch pieces simply and easily. If a band saw is not available, a lumber company will usually cut them for a reasonable price; or they may be cut out with a saber saw or a small keyhole saw.

Building the Arch

Several methods may be followed in building the arches into the flats. The quickest and easiest method is described here.

For a door arch, the cross rail which forms the top of the door is removed or omitted. The two lower ends of the arch pieces then rest directly on top of the sides of the door, as shown in Figure 35. The rail which is normally placed at the top of the door opening is then placed so that it rests on top of the arch. Two short rails are cut to fit between the arched opening and the sides of the flat where the arch joins the sides of the door. The rail that rests on top of the arch is fastened with keystones to the side of the flat. At the center of the rail, the two pieces of the arch and the rail are held together by a triangle.

Proportional Enlargement

Frequently, the arches in a set vary in size. If the tops of the arches

FIG. 35.—FLAT WITH ARCH

are round, there is no problem. If, however, the set design calls for other types of arches, there is a problem of height in proportion to width. The solution to this problem is proportional enlargement.

For example, on the same set there may be one door 3 feet wide with an arch 2 feet high from the start of the curve. Another door may be 5 feet wide. The height of the arch of this door will not be automatically 2 times as high—or even 1½ times as high—as the first door; the height of the arch increases in direct proportion to the width of the door.

There is a simple method for determining increase in height in proportion to increase in width. An oblong is drawn the exact size, or half the size, of the arch. (See Figure 36.) Next, a diagonal is drawn from corner to corner of the oblong and extended beyond the upper corner. The base of the rectangle is extended to the size of the new arch, and a line is erected from the new base line to intersect the diagonal. The rectangle is completed, and the new arch is drawn. The new arch will be in the same proportion as the first arch.

Third Dimension for Arches

To give the actual third dimension required for some sets, arches must have thickness—an effect not possible with the old-fashioned method of painting depth in perspective. Such thickness should be built as a separate piece which may be attached or removed at will. However, this thickness may be built directly to the arch, though the piece will then require more storage space.

Another arch must be cut. Next, pieces of 1 by 3 inch lumber are cut to length according to the thickness desired. These pieces are nailed between the two arch pieces to hold them apart. Then straight

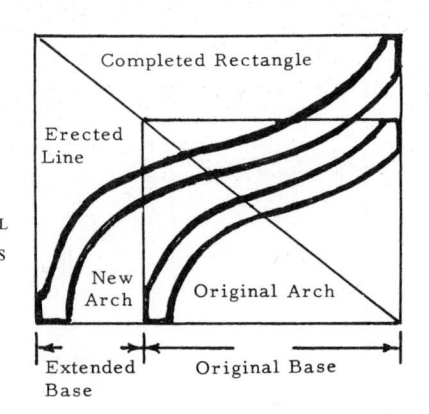

FIG. 36.—PROPORTIONAL
ENLARGEMENT OF ARCHES

Completed Rectangle

Erected
Line

New
Arch

Original Arch

Extended
Base

Original Base

pieces are attached to form the side pieces of the door opening. (See Figure 37.)

When the framework is finished, a piece of cloth about six inches wider than the thickness of the arch is tacked around the arch, with a loose edge of the cloth projecting about 3 inches on each side. This loose edge must be split at frequent intervals to fit the curve of the arch and glued to the framework, front and back.

BUILDING SET PIECES

All other types of scenery are built on the same principle as the flats. It is just a question of difference of size and shape. For example, a set rock starts out as a flat; it ends up as a flat with irregular edges. This irregularity is called profile. (See Figure 38.)

Profile Scenery

The material used to make the profile may be pressed wood, Beaverboard, or ¼ inch three-ply veneer. Veneer is the best material for this purpose; Beaverboard is the cheapest, easiest to cut, and the least serviceable.

The construction of profile pieces is very simple. A frame or flat is built as large as is possible to include the shape of the rock. The frame may be square, rectangular, or even triangular, depending

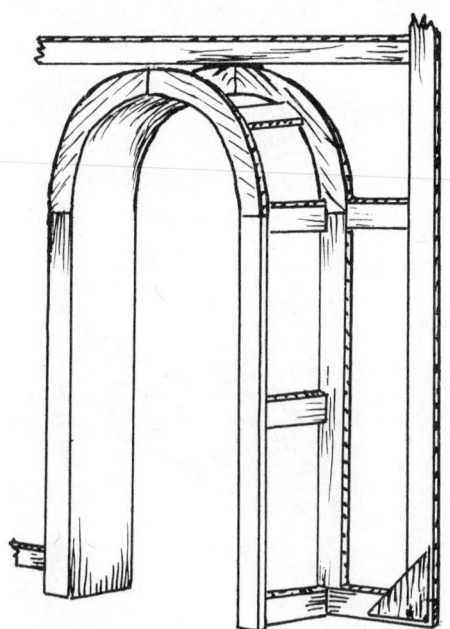

FIG. 37.—THIRD DIMENSION FOR ARCHES

upon the shape required. Then the profile material is attached to the side of the flat opposite the keystones and corners, as shown in Figure 38.

Beaverboard and pressed wood may be attached with blued lath nails. Veneer is attached with 1¼ inch clout nails. The nails must be clinched on the reverse side of the flat.

Cloth is tacked to the frame around the inside edge. The muslin should be large enough to cover the profile. The cloth is then glued to the frame and to the profiled edges. When the glue is thoroughly dry, the outline of the rock may be drawn on the profile and cut, or, perhaps better still, the rock may be painted and the edges cut after the paint is dry.

This same method of construction may be used for a variety of other objects, such as shrubbery, bushes, small trees, horizon lines, and house tops.

A cheap, easy to use, though not very substantial, substitute for the profile pieces described above is corrugated cardboard. This material may be purchased from a box factory or secured, usually free of charge, from stores that receive merchandise packed in large cartons. Corrugated board requires some bracing with lumber, but it is sturdy, takes paint well, and it is easily cut with a knife. The cracks in corrugated board may be covered with masking tape or gummed tape.

Fireplaces

Fireplaces, regardless of style or design, are built on the same principle as other scenery: from frames of 1 by 3 inch lumber held together by keystones and corners and covered with cloth. They are

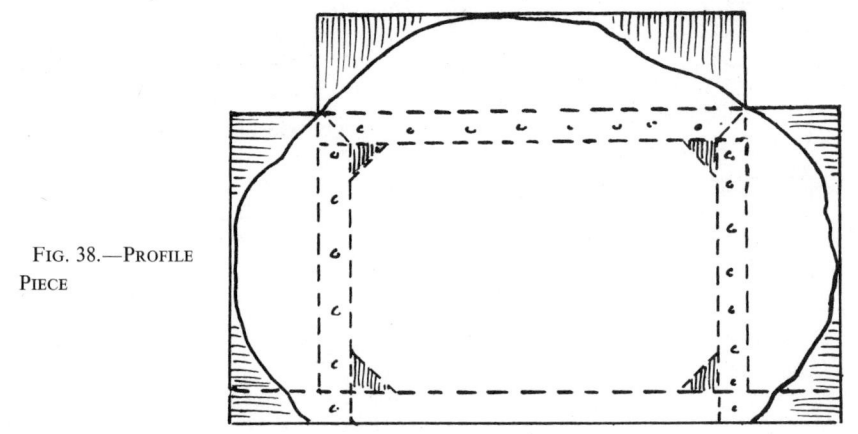

FIG. 38.—PROFILE PIECE

usually built on one of two general plans: (1) a flat facing which is placed against a piece of scenery, such as a door, in which there is an opening for the firebox, and (2) built out to stand away from the wall in sufficient thickness so that the firebox and fireplace are complete in one piece. (See Figures 39 and 40.)

An average size for fireplaces is 4 to 6 feet wide by 4 to 4½ feet high to the mantel. The firebox opening is at least 2 feet square.

The flat type.—The flat type is frequently a framework approximately 4 feet wide by 7 feet high, with the mantel at the suggested height—4½ feet—and the rest of the frame projecting above the mantel. The firebox opening is of course at the bottom. (See Figure 39.) Such a fireplace may be placed in front of a door flat; then the flat serves two purposes. The opening of the door provides the opening of the firebox. Two small flats are hinged together and placed back of the door opening to form the firebox. The face of the flat-type fireplace may be trimmed with a variety of moldings to give a more finished effect, as shown in Figure 39.

The built-out type.—The built-out type of fireplace is constructed of two frames held apart with pieces of 1 by 3 inch lumber, the length of which is determined by the thickness of the fireplace or, rather, by the depth of the firebox. The framework is covered with cloth: front, ends, and inside the firebox. A mantel is placed on top of the frame-

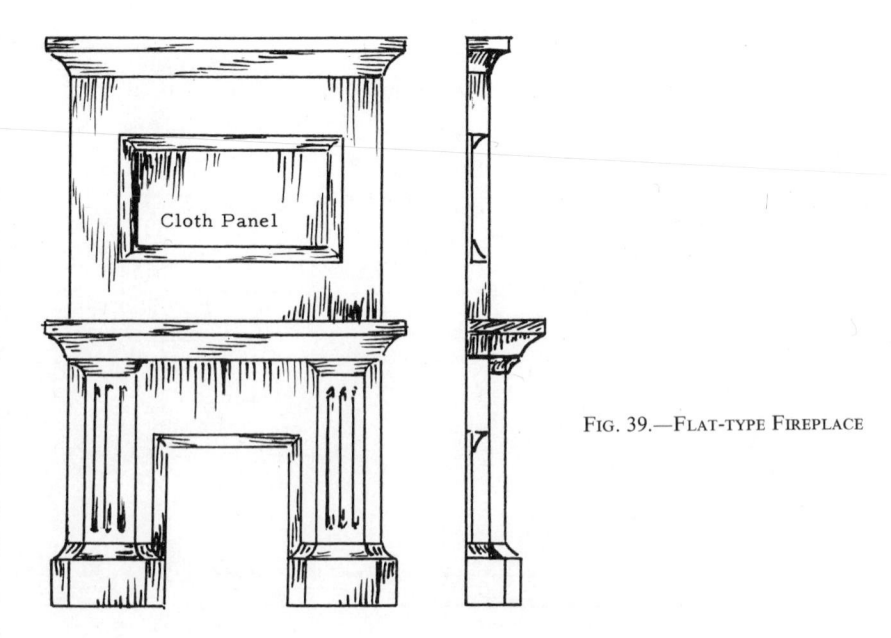

Cloth Panel

FIG. 39.—FLAT-TYPE FIREPLACE

work. The face of this type of fireplace also may be trimmed with molding. (See Figure 40.)

Door Backings

A backing is used in back of doors or other openings. It is constructed of two or more small flats, usually 4 feet wide and 10 feet high, hinged together. When they are opened, they stand in an inverted L-shape or in an inverted U-shape. The flats are usually covered separately and then placed edge to edge and hinged together on the front with back flap hinges placed at the top, center, and bottom as described in Chapter 2.

Pillars

Sometimes such objects as pillars, trees, stumps, and rocks must be built, either in half- or full-round. Pillars are constructed by using half- or full-circles, which are covered with lattice strips, clothed with muslin, and glued, just as in the flats described above. (See Figure 41.)

The number of circles required depends upon the height of the pillar. A circle is placed approximately every 3 or 4 feet. The circles are held together by one or more battens, which extend the full length of the pillar. Lattice strips are nailed around the circles ½ to 1 inch apart.

Large cardboard shipping tubes may be used in place of the wooden framework covered with cloth. The effect of fluting on columns may be obtained with painted vertical stripes or with a series of half-round strips nailed around the column. Either will be effective.

Trees

Tree trunks are constructed in much the same manner as pillars.

FIG. 40.—BUILT-OUT FIREPLACE

The main difference is that instead of being built around circles tree trunks are built around irregular shaped pieces so that the tree will not look round. Also, the bottom of the tree is usually somewhat larger than the top.

A tree is sometimes shaped with a combination of lattice strips and ¼ inch mesh heavy galvanized sanding screen (hardware cloth) shaped around the trunk. Chicken wire (poultry netting) may be used, but it is not as substantial. (See Figure 42.)

The framework of the trunk is covered in one of several ways. A cover may be stretched tightly around the tree, tacked and glued

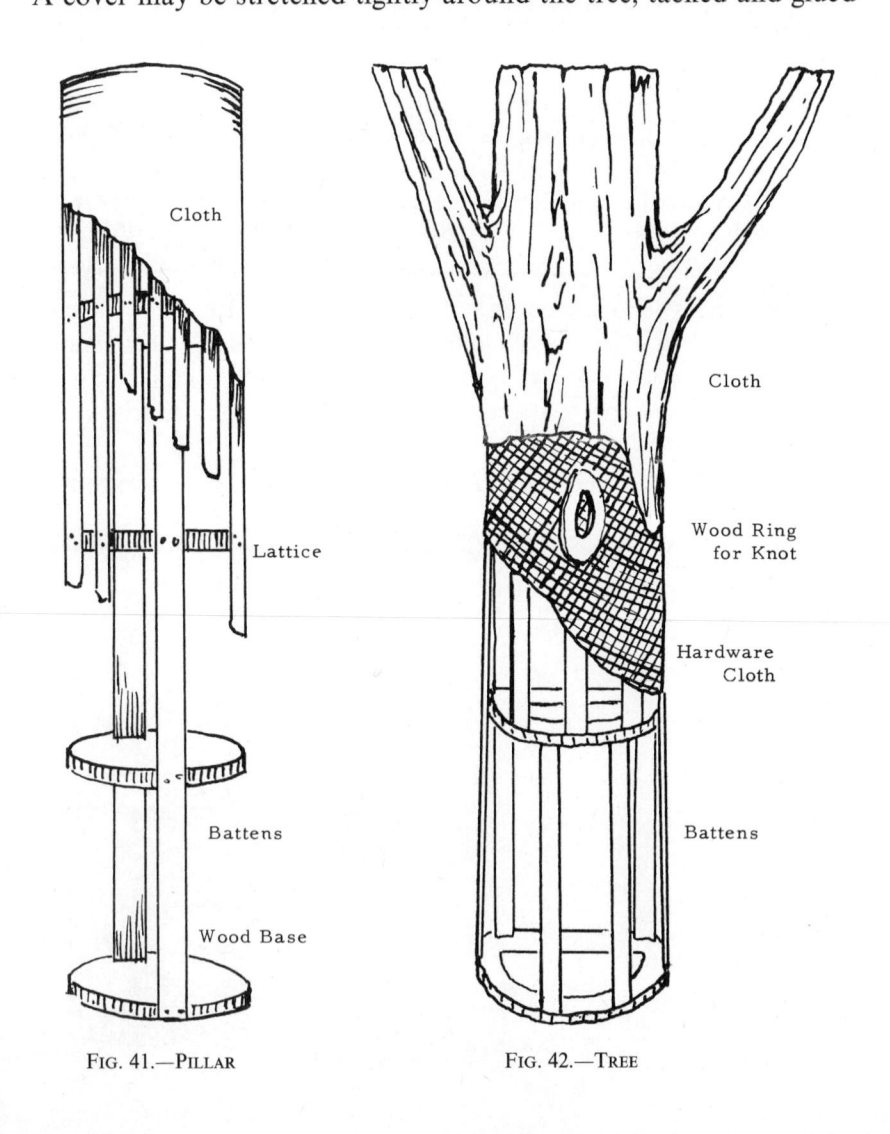

FIG. 41.—PILLAR   FIG. 42.—TREE

to the frame, and then more crushed and wrinkled cloth tacked and glued to the foundation, or the crushed and wrinkled cloth may be put on immediately without the foundation. The crushed cloth gives the appearance of bark.

A tree stump is made in exactly the same way as a tree. The under framework of the tree stump, however, should be sufficiently rigid to allow the stump to be used as a seat if the action of the play demands it.

Rocks

Rocks are built around a box-shaped framework. The amount of under construction will depend on whether or not the rocks must support the weight of actors during the performance. The under construction need not necessarily be exceedingly heavy; sufficient under-bracing is necessary only to keep the wire which is put over the wood from bending out of shape. (See Figure 43.)

After the box-shaped framework has been constructed, irregular pieces of wood are attached to it until the framework takes on the semblance of the rock shape desired. Then hardware cloth (or chicken wire) is shaped around the framework and stapled to it. The construction should be checked for weak places where the wire may be too easily bent out of shape with use during the performance. Then the rock is covered with muslin, glued, and painted.

Trees, stumps, and rocks should be thoroughly painted with scene paint or dry color containing more glue than is commonly used. This will help harden and stiffen the surface. The additional glue should not be added to the paint used on columns because it may cause warping.

CEILING FLATS

The depth of the average ceiling is 16 feet; the width varies ac-

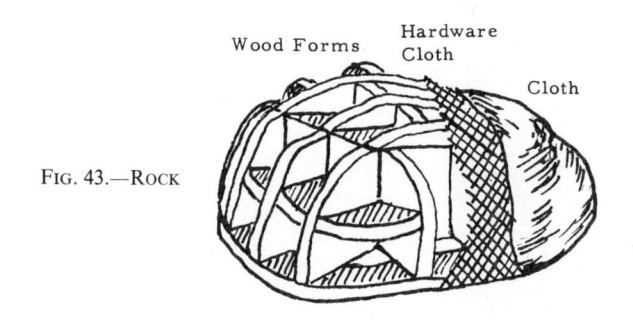

Wood Forms   Hardware Cloth

Cloth

FIG. 43.—ROCK

cording to the size of the proscenium opening. A ceiling is a framework of 1 by 3 inch lumber built to hold a covering of unbleached muslin. It may be constructed as a permanent flat to hang in place at all times. More commonly, however, it is built to fold and roll. There are two reasons for this type of construction. In the first place, a ceiling is very large, and if built in one piece it would present difficulty in storing. In the second place, it would be impossible to remove a piece that size from the stage.

Folding Ceiling

A folding ceiling is constructed in the following manner: Five or seven 1 by 3 inch battens are cut the depth of the desired finished ceiling (usually 16 feet). On each end of these battens ceiling irons are attached. (A ceiling iron is a thin metal plate with five screw holes in one end, by which it is attached to the batten, and a bolt hole in the other end. In the center of the ceiling iron, between the screw holes and the bolt hole, there is an iron ring.) Next, four battens are cut to half the entire width of the ceiling. These four battens are then hinged together in pairs with 6-inch strap hinges to form two long battens.

To assemble the folding ceiling, the two long battens are placed 16 feet apart hinge down on the stage and the short battens placed equidistant between the long battens. The pieces are bolted together with bolts and wing nuts which pass through the long battens and the ceiling irons on the short battens. (See Figure 44.) The frame, fairly rigid in construction, is now ready for clothing.

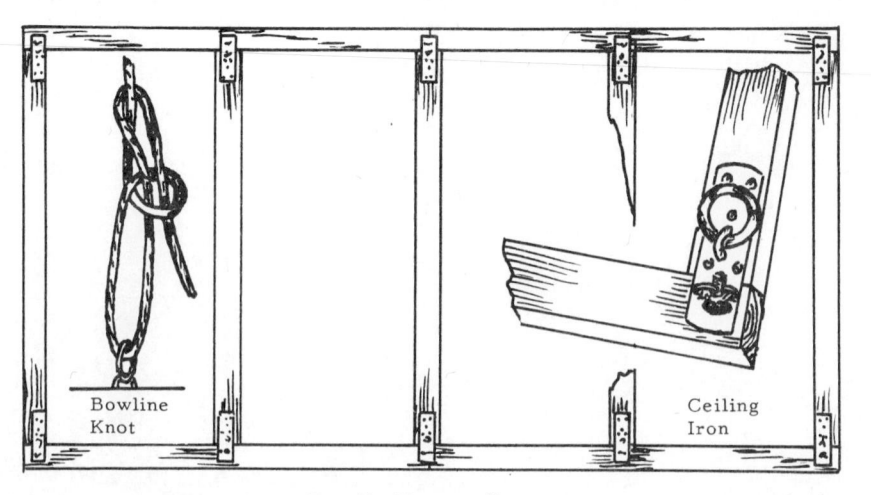

Bowline
Knot

Ceiling
Iron

FIG. 44.—FOLDING CEILING

Unbleached muslin strips sufficient to make a cloth the depth of the ceiling and about a foot longer than the width are sewed together. The seams run the long way, or width, of the ceiling. The cloth is tacked to the two long battens on the hinged side and glued, exactly as in making regular flats. However, here the additional cloth at the ends is taken around the ends to the back, where it is tacked to the two end battens but not fastened permanently. When the glue is dry, the ceiling is ready for painting.

To fold the ceiling, the tacks are removed from the two end battens first. Then the cross battens are removed and the cloth is folded with the painted surfaces together. Then it may be rolled for transportation or storage. To assemble, the cloth is unfolded or unrolled, the battens are replaced, and the cloth is again tacked to the end battens.

Book Ceiling

Another type of ceiling is the book ceiling. This ceiling is made of two frames instead of one. The two parts of the book ceiling may be constructed as permanent pieces—in other words, like ordinary flats —or made to fold and roll, like the folding ceiling.

The two pieces are each constructed the width of the stage and half the depth and hinged together. The hinges—about five in all— are placed on the cloth side. The cloth covers the hinges and the crack between the two pieces.

A set of lines is attached to three ceiling irons across the center of the book ceiling, as well as to the front and back. When the center set of lines is lifted the ceiling closes like a book, and the ceiling may be raised clear of the set even when the loft is not very high. (See Figure 45.)

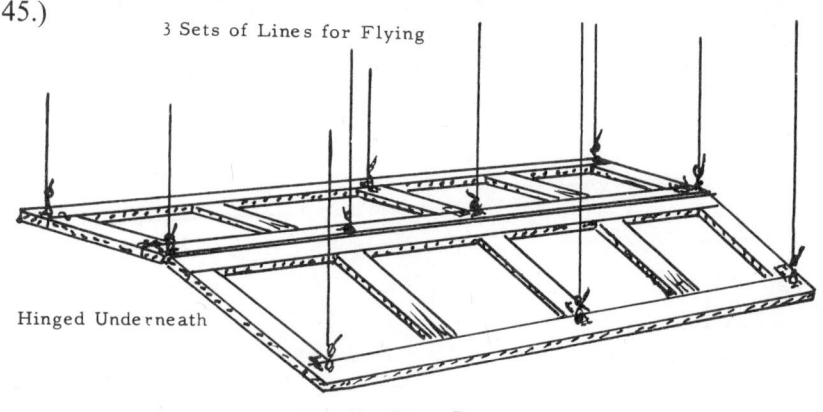

FIG. 45.—BOOK CEILING

5

STAIRS AND PLATFORMS

Stairways and platforms are of the greatest importance in stagecraft, and they are the pieces of scenery on which amateurs most often make mistakes.

STAIRS

Steps are made up of the rise, or riser, the run, or tread, and the stringers. The rise is the distance that one steps up. The tread is the part upon which one steps. The stringers are the notched boards to which the risers and treads are attached.

Height of the Rise

In step construction the relationship between the rise and the tread is very important. Before this relationship can be determined and the stringer cut, the height of the parallel, or support, to which the stairway is attached must be determined. (See the discussion of parallels and platforms below.) It is usually possible to determine arbitrarily the height of supports on the stage. Therefore, it is advisable to build parallels and platforms an even number of feet high, or at least an even number of inches, so that the rise of each step can be made 6 inches—the average step height.

Width of the Tread

The width of the tread varies in direct relationship to the height of the rise. There is a simple formula for determining this relationship: $2R + T = 24$ inches, where R is the rise dimension and T the tread dimension. For example, if it has been determined that the rise is to be 6 inches, to determine the width of the tread multiply the rise (R) by 2 and subtract the result from 24. In this instance, $2R = 12$; $24 - 12 = 12$, the width of the tread for this particular rise. If the rise is 7 inches, then 2 times 7 is 14 which subtracted from 24 leaves 10, the width of the tread for that particular rise.

Cutting the Stringer

With the rise and the tread established, the stringer may be cut. The stringer is usually cut from 1 by 12 inch clear pine board. Into the board a series of right-angle notches is cut to form the steps.

Note that the stringer will contain one less notch than the number of steps required. For example, six risers of 6 inches each will be needed for a 3-foot stairway, but only five notches will be required to form the stringer for this stairway.

The notches are drawn on the board with a steel square or with any square object large enough to measure 6 inches on one side and 12 inches on the other side (the rise and tread of the average-size step). It is very important that each of the steps be exactly the same and that due allowance be made for the first rise and last tread. If the rise is 6 inches, then the first riser will be cut 5¼ inches (assuming that ¾ inch lumber is used throughout). If the tread is 12 inches, the last tread is cut only 11¼ inches wide. (See Figure 46.)

The number of stringers needed for stairs varies according to the width of the stairs. A stair 3 feet wide will require only two stringers —one at each side. For wider stairs, an additional stringer is needed for every additional 3 or 4 feet of width.

Assembling the Stair

After the stringers are cut the risers are nailed into place with six-penny or eightpenny cement-coated nails. Next, the treads are nailed to the stringer and to the front edge of the treads beneath them. Then the risers are nailed from the back to the back edges of the treads to strengthen the steps. (See Figure 47.)

Adding Tread Overhang

For many types of stairs the tread should project beyond the riser.

FIG. 46.—CUTTING THE STRINGER

Such projection is called overhang, or, technically, the nose. The simplest way of getting this effect is by attaching to the face of the square-edged stair pieces of molding called nose and cove. Nose and cove molding is inexpensive; it may be obtained at any lumber company. (See Figure 48.)

Attaching Stairs to Platforms

There are several methods of holding stairways in place on the stage. The simplest method is the method of hooking the stair to the platform shown in Figure 47. A notch just large enough to allow a 1 by 3 inch strip of lumber to be nailed across the stair from side to side is cut into each stringer below the back edge of the upper tread. To this piece of lumber there are attached either two halves of a 6-inch strap hinge or two stage brace cleats. Another strip of 1 by 3 inch lumber is nailed to the parallel supporting the platform, and the half-hinges or brace cleats attached to the stringers are slipped over this piece as shown in Figure 47 to hold the stair firmly in place.

Stair Rails

The stair rail or banister, if required, is made as a separate piece which may be attached to the stair or removed at will. The piece consists of the newel post, balusters, rungs or rounds, hand rail, and a triangular piece to mask the space between the steps and the floor.

In building this unit, a stringer is cut just like the one used for the steps. To it are attached narrow strips of lumber similar to risers and treads, and to these strips are attached newel posts and rungs. Nose

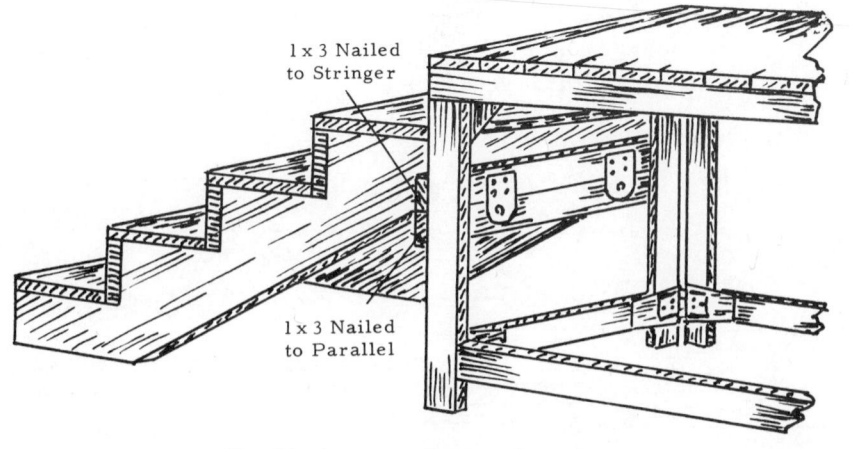

1 x 3 Nailed
to Stringer

1 x 3 Nailed
to Parallel

FIG. 47.—ATTACHING STAIR TO PARALLEL

and cove molding may be used around the ends of the treads if it has been used on the steps. To mask the space between the steps and the floor, two pieces of 1 by 3 inch lumber are attached to the stringer across the bottom and up the side. These two pieces form the two right angles of a triangle, with the stringer forming the hypotenuse. (See Figure 48.) Plywood triangles and clout nails are used in constructing this masking piece just as in constructing a flat, and the triangular unit is covered with cloth.

The railing may need to be only a few inches wide; or it may be as much as a foot wide to hold an elaborately curved hand rail. In some cases stair rails or banisters may be almost a small set of steps and may require two stringers to hold the treads, risers, and banisters in place. Regardless of the size and design, the piece is bolted or hinged to the regular step.

If bolts are used, the stringer of the railing is placed on the stringer of the step and two or more holes approximately ⅜ inch in diameter are drilled through the two stringers. Three-eighths inch bolts are slipped through the holes and are held in place with wing nuts, which can be tightened with thumb and finger. If loose-pin hinges are used, one or more hinges are placed on the risers or on the treads, half the hinge on the steps and the other half on the railing. (See Figure 49.) When the railing is attached to the stairs, the hinges are slipped together and a piece of wire is passed through the two halves of the

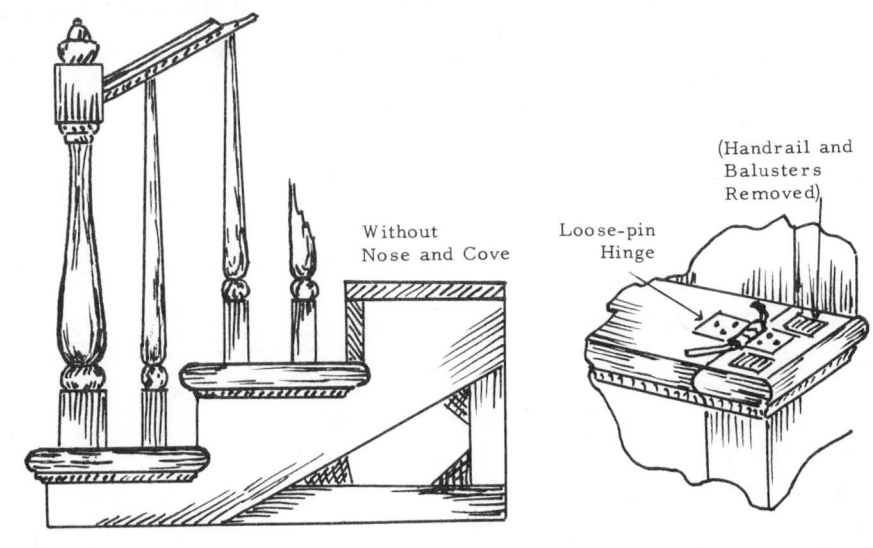

Without
Nose and Cove

Loose-pin
Hinge

(Handrail and
Balusters
Removed)

FIG. 48—STAIR RAILING   FIG. 49.—HINGING THE RAILING TO THE STEP

hinge to hold it together. The wire is removed easily when the steps and railing are taken apart.

A variety of rails may be attached to one set of steps. Also, the railing may be made for either the right or the left of the stage, depending upon where the steps are set. Even if this kind of facing is not used, the triangular piece masking the space between the steps and the floor should be constructed. Without the railing, the triangular piece fits under the stringer of the step and is held in place with loose-pin hinges.

PLATFORMS

Quite as important as the stairway is the platform. A platform is made up of two separate pieces: the parallel—the box-like structure which supports the platform—and the platform, which is simply the cover which fits over the parallel.

The parallel is made up of four or more flat-like frames. The frames are hinged together so that the parallel may be opened to support the platform or folded flat for storage. There are several methods of building the frames and hinging them together. The method described below is the simplest and quickest.

Material for the Parallel

The frames are made of 1 by 3 inch common pine. If the parallel is small and very low special attention need not be given to the quality of the lumber except to see that it is reasonably free of knots. If the parallel is very large and high great care should be taken in selecting clear, strong lumber.

Size of the Parallel

Some consideration should be given to the size of the parallels and platforms so that they will be flexible in use. That is, they should be sized so that if additional ones are built they will fit and work together interchangeably. Therefore, when the size of the completed parallel has been decided upon the size of the pieces of the frame may be computed.

Allowance must be made for the thickness of the lumber in computing the over-all height of the parallel and platform. Ordinarily, ¾ inch lumber is used. Since the platform fits on top of the parallel the height of the parallel must be ¾ inch less than the over-all height of the parallel and platform, and the width of the pieces must be 2½ inches less than the dimensions of the platform. For example, if the width of the platform is 4 feet, two sides of the parallel must be 3 feet 9½ inches; if the length of the platform is 6 feet, the other two sides of the parallel must be 5 feet 9½ inches.

The Sides of the Parallel

The top rails of the parallel must run the full length of the sides of the frames and rest on the upright legs. (See Figure 50.) The bottom rail of each side piece is placed between the two legs, usually the width of a 1 by 3 inch piece of lumber from the bottom. The frames are held together like flats with keystones and corners. The corners are set flush with the edge of the sides and down ¾ inch from the top. The bottom rail is held by two keystones set flush with the edge, as shown in Figure 50.

Additional supports may be necessary on the long sides of the parallel. If so, a center brace may be added between the top and bottom rails. The brace is attached to the top rail with a keystone set down ¾ inch from the edge. In order to carry the weight on down to the floor a piece of 1 by 3 inch lumber about 6 inches long is placed beneath the bottom rail. The 6-inch batten, the bottom rail, and the center brace are held together with a keystone, as shown in Figure 50.

If the parallel is very long, one or more additional frames should be placed crosswise inside the parallel. The inside frames are constructed in the same manner as the sides but they are ¾ inch lower than the sides.

Corner Bracing

To prevent side sway in high parallels it is necessary to add corner

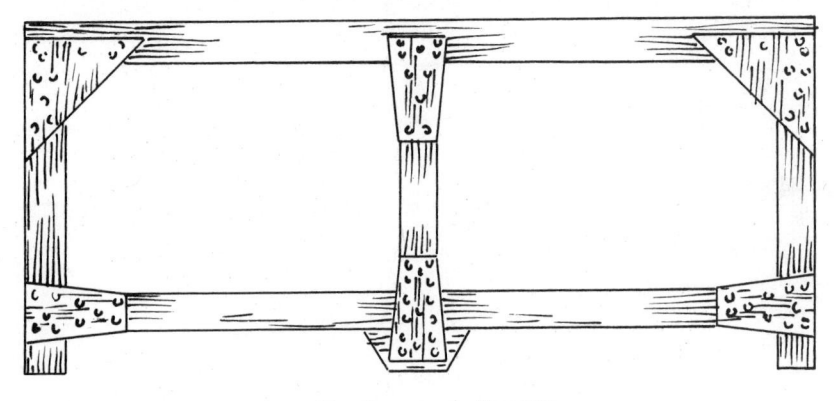

FIG. 50.—SIDE OF THE PARALLEL

braces to each of the four sides. These corner braces are pieces of 1 by 3 inch lumber cut long enough to reach from the middle of the top rail down to about the center of the side stile. The ends of the brace are cut at a 45 degree angle, and the brace is held in place by triangles placed flush at the sides and down ¾ inch from the top. (See Figure 51.)

Assembling the Parallel

To assemble the parallel the completed frames are placed side by side, keystones and corners up, and hinged together with 2-inch tight-pin backflap hinges. For greater stability of the parallel it is advisable to fasten the hinges to the side stiles with four screws and two ³⁄₁₆ inch flathead stove bolts. Two hinges per corner are sufficient for low parallels—one placed on the triangle at the top and the other on the keystone at the bottom. Three hinges may be necessary for high parallels.

After the four side pieces have been hinged together the outer two ends are brought together and hinged to complete the four sides of the parallel. The easiest method of joining this fourth corner is to, first, remove the screws from the hinges on one side of any of the frames already fastened. Next, place the unhinged edges together and hinge them. Then return the screws to the old holes along the edge from which the hinges were removed. The hinges will then be on each inside corner of the parallel, and it is absolutely certain that the parallel will fold flat in either direction and that the space in all four corners is equal.

If an inside frame is used in the parallel, it is hinged first to one side with tight-pin backflap hinges. If the hinges are placed on the side of the center piece on which the keystones and corners have been

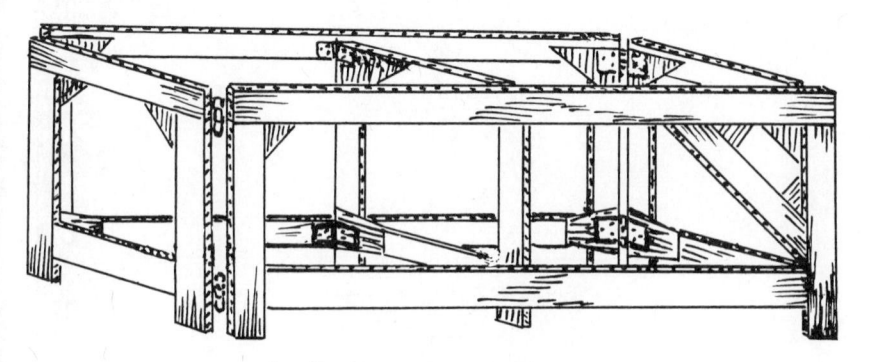

FIG. 51.—THE ASSEMBLED PARALLEL

placed, then at the other end of the inside frame the hinges are attached to the side opposite the keystones and corners. Next, the parallel is folded flat, and the location of the hinges on the outside parallel is marked. Then the parallel is opened, and the hinges are attached. If the inside frame is attached carefully, it will fold flat with the rest of the parallel. (See Figure 51.)

Building the Platform

A number of methods and materials may be used in constructing platforms. The cheapest and most satisfactory material is 4-inch or 6-inch matched fir flooring (tongue and groove), either edge grain or flat grain. The platform is constructed by nailing the fir flooring to a number of strips or battens of 1 by 3 inch clear pine. The number of battens required varies with the width of the platform. Three are sufficient for a platform 4 feet wide. For maximum strength, the flooring should run across the short way of the platform and the 1 by 3 inch battens the long way. (See Figure 52.)

In constructing the platform, the battens are cut just long enough to fit inside the parallel. Then they are laid out to conform to the inside dimensions of the parallel so that when the flooring is attached ¾ inch of flooring projects beyond the battens on all four sides. (See Figure 52.) Before the first piece of flooring is attached the groove is removed to give the edge of the platform a flat surface. Then the flooring is nailed to the battens through the tongue with fourpenny cement-coated nails, as shown in Figure 53. This is standard practice in laying matched floors. It may be advisable to turn the finished platform over and nail again from the under side.

When the platform is finished, the battens should just slip inside

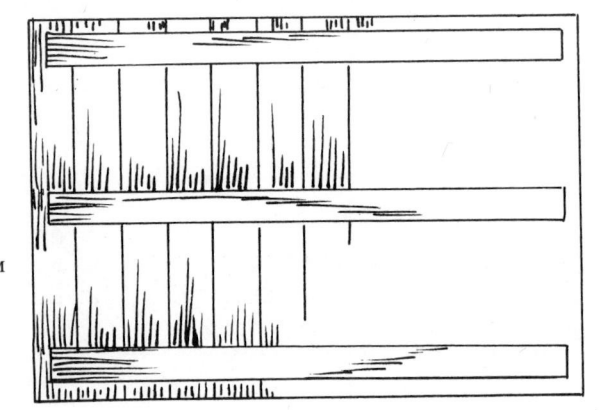

FIG. 52.—THE PLATFORM

the parallel, and the flooring should rest on the top of the parallel flush with the outside of the parallel on all four sides. Three-quarter inch plywood may be used in place of flooring. This is less work, but the platform tends to be springy.

Holding the Parallel and Platform

The 1 by 3 inch battens prevent the parallel from collapsing inward. To prevent the parallel from spreading outward loose-pin hinges may be attached to the inside of the upper rail of the parallel and to the bottom of the platform. A simpler and equally effective method is to drive a sixpenny nail through the platform into the center of the top rail in each of the four sides. These four nails are adequate to hold the platform in place and prevent spreading. When the platform is taken off the nails are easily removed.

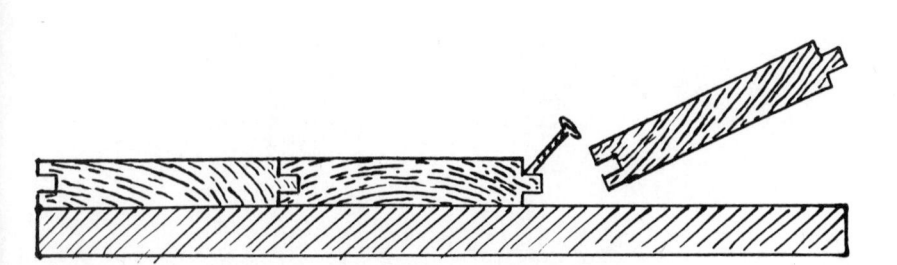

Fig. 53.—Nailing Tongue-and-Groove Flooring

6

DOORS AND WINDOWS

Except for minor details, the process of building doors and windows is the same. The average width of doors and windows is 30 inches. A door must be at least 6½ feet high. The height of the window varies with the height of the door, and both vary with the design of the set.

It is difficult to build a door which will not warp and sag out of shape. Then, too, smooth operation of a door is so vitally important to the play that it is not wise to use homemade makeshifts. An inexpensive, lightweight, regular factory-built door costs little more than the material required to build one. The most practical door for stage use is made of 1⅜ inch soft pine.

It is quite possible to build windows, since the smooth operation expected of doors is not required of them. Window construction is described below.

The Door

A stage door consists of not only the door itself but also the jamb and casing. The jamb is the box-like frame into which the door fits. The casing is the trim around the jamb. The jamb and casing are usually made of 1 by 4 inch pine, not necessarily select lumber.

The Jamb

The jamb is made of four pieces: two pieces of 1 by 4 inch lumber approximately 4 inches longer than the height of the door and one piece each of 1 by 3 inch lumber and 1 by 4 inch lumber, both ½ inch longer than the width of the door.

The 1 by 3 inch piece, which forms the door sill, is grooved with a 1 by ¼ inch groove its full length and nailed between the two uprights, flush with the bottom and the front edge of the jamb, with the groove down. The 1 by 4 inch piece forms the head jamb. It is nailed

69

at the top between the two uprights. The distance between the head jamb and door sill should be ¾ inch more than the height of the door. If properly assembled, the two sides of the jamb will project 1¾ inches above the head jamb. (See Figure 54.)

The Casing

The two upright sides of the casing are cut ¼ inch longer than the distance from the bottom of the door sill to the inside of the door jamb. These pieces are nailed in place to the jamb, at right angles to the jamb and set back from the inside of the jamb about ¼ inch. The head casing is cut the width of the casing, from outside edge to outside edge of the side pieces, and nailed into place, set back ¼ inch from the top of the jamb.

Door Iron

Door Iron

Fig. 54.—Door Jamb   Fig. 55.—Door Casing

A decorative molding may be added to the outside edge of the casing to give a more finished appearance to the door and additional strength. Also, the frame may be reinforced at the back with a number of angle irons or wood blocks. (See Figure 55.)

The Door Iron

The door iron is placed in the groove in the bottom of the door sill. It is a piece of band iron ¾ by ³⁄₁₆ inches. It is cut long enough to run up the sides of the frame about 8 inches, and it should be either bolted or screwed to the frame. (See Figure 55.)

Hanging the Door

The door is hung 1¼ inches off of the floor and hinged flush with the back edge of the jamb. For stage doors it is not necessary to countersink the hinges into the door and jamb, although this may be done. Three-inch loose-pin butt hinges are usually used for this purpose.

Since the jamb has been constructed ½ inch wider and ¾ inch higher than the door—inside measurements, side to side and sill to head jamb—there will be ¼ inch clearance on each side of the door, ¼ inch at the top, and ½ inch clearance between the bottom of the door and the sill. A stage door should not fit tightly.

The door stop.—When the hinges are in place, the door should be closed and temporarily nailed shut. The door stop is then nailed into place. There is special molding for this purpose. It is nailed to the jamb at both sides and the top, as shown in Figure 56. The stop prevents the door from swinging through the jamb.

The lock.—All locks include door knobs. Mortised locks may be used on stage doors, but rim locks are more practical. The rim lock is attached to the back of the door, rather than fitted into the door. It operates better than the mortised lock for stage purposes, it is easier to install, less apt to get out of adjustment, and it is inexpensive. (See Figures 56, 58.)

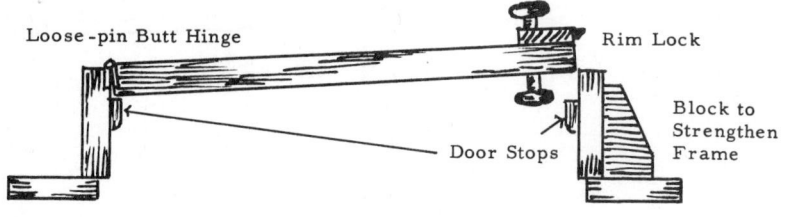

FIG. 56.—CROSS SECTION OF DOOR AND FRAME

THE WINDOW

Jamb and Casing

Window jamb and casing differ only slightly from door jamb and casing. Instead of a 1 by 3 inch piece across the bottom a 1 by 4 inch piece is used, and the casing across the bottom is set flush with the jamb. A molding may be added to give the effect of overhang of the window sill. (See Figure 57.)

Depending upon the desired design, the window may be hinged to swing like a casement, constructed to raise and lower, or built not to open at all. If the window is hinged, a stop is used around the jamb, as in door construction. If the window must raise and lower two stops must be used to form a groove in which the window slides. A window which must be raised and lowered should be built to fit tightly enough to stay without any device to hold it open when it is raised.

Window Glass

If a window must be made of a number of small panes, the dividing pieces, or mullions, may be held in place with corrugated fasten-

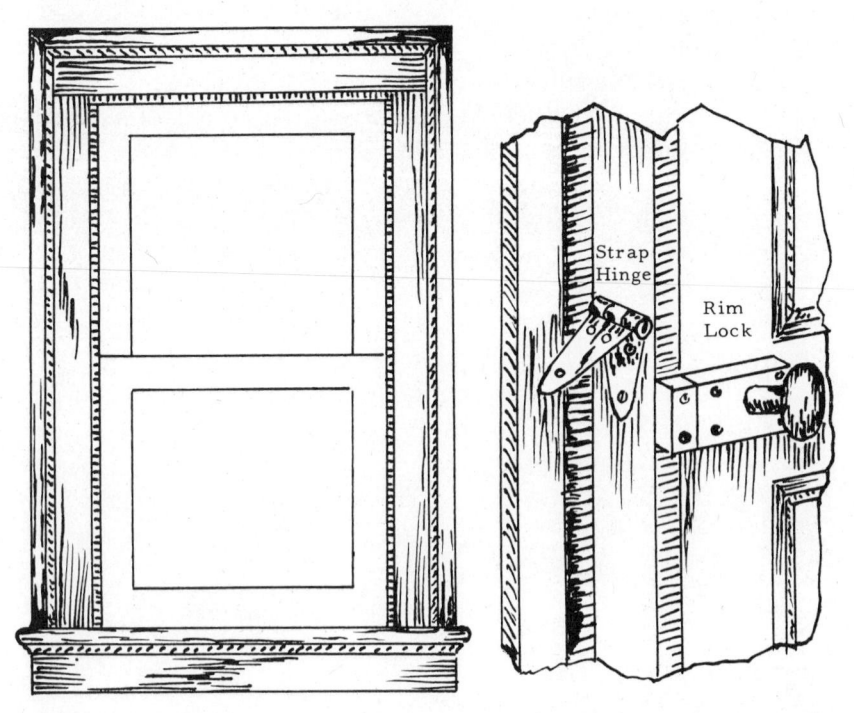

FIG. 57.—STAGE WINDOW   FIG. 58.—HOLDING A DOOR IN THE SET

ers or, better, with fine finishing nails. Most stage windows are covered on the back with pearl window screen. This screen strengthens the window, gives the effect of glass, makes the window opening look less like a hole, and, equally important, prevents actors from sticking their heads through what is supposed to be glass. Clear heavy sheet plastic may also be used.

Double and French Doors

Double doors and French doors are built on the same principle as single doors. French doors should be purchased ready-made, unglazed. However, it is possible to build a fairly acceptable French door. When double doors are used, one door is usually arranged to be closed first and has a stop along its edge for the other door. This stop may be purchased from a lumber company. It is called an astragal.

Holding Doors and Windows in Sets

There are several ways of holding doors and windows in place in flats. The simplest, most commonly-used way is to attach the lower half of a 6-inch strap hinge to the outside of the jamb, close to the back of the casing. The upper half of the hinge is allowed to swing free. When the door or window is inserted, the hinge is held up, and when the door is in place the hinge drops down and holds the door tightly to the door frame in the flat. (See Figure 58.)

In addition, the flat on each side of the door or window is usually braced with stage braces. In some instances jacks may be used. (See Chapter 2.)

7

PROPERTIES AND SOUND EFFECTS

Properties

Properties are so numerous and so varied that no rules or suggestions could cover the entire field. In addition to the difficulty involved in securing properties there is also the problem of caring for them during the performance, for every prop must be in exactly the right place at the right moment or the play may be ruined. For these reasons properties should be handled with infinite pains and with great ingenuity. Furthermore, properties should be put away or covered between performances, and they should never be handled by anyone not in charge of them. Stage furniture should only be used by actors during performances.

Almost everything on the set except the actual scenery comes under the head of properties, or props—furniture, draperies, pictures, rugs, rocks, stumps, flowers, food. In addition to these general properties there are hand props. They are the articles the actors use in the action of the play: dishes, books, papers, cigarettes, watches, handkerchiefs, etc. Some properties are standard stage equipment; others must be borrowed, rented, purchased, or made especially for each play.

Ground Cloth

Most common of all properties is the ground cloth, which is simply a piece of canvas large enough to cover the acting area of the stage. The ground cloth is tacked to the stage floor before the production is set and taken up after the run of the show. Rugs or carpets may be used in addition to the ground cloth. In some cases a carpet may take the place of a ground cloth.

Furniture

Furniture for rehearsal is often as much of a problem as furniture for a performance. Simple rehearsal furniture may be built easily; it may even be used in the production of plays requiring crude tables and benches. For this kind of furniture, the legs of the tables and benches are made of 2-inch plank, the top and edges of 1-inch lumber. The size of the pieces may vary with the need, but the height of the benches and chairs and tables is fairly standard. A bench or chair is usually 18 inches high, a table 30 inches.

Construction is simple. The legs are cut and the top nailed to the legs with eightpenny cement-coated nails. Then a band of 1 by 3 inch lumber is attached to the top and to the legs. A crosspiece of 1 by 3 inch lumber is fastened from leg to leg, about a foot from the bottom, to add strength. Tables and benches are made in exactly the same way. (See Figure 59.)

There is another simple type of table or chair construction which allows for greater variety in design. This type requires four separate legs, four rails, and a top. The legs and rails are held together at each corner with two small blocks screwed to the legs and rails. (See Figure 60.) After the bottom is assembled, the top is nailed to the legs and rails. The size and shape of the legs and rails will vary with the type of furniture that is being built.

Soft wood may be used, and the finished pieces may be painted or stained. Furniture—and other objects that are to be handled—may also be painted with casein or rubber-base paint. If a glossy effect is desired, furniture may be painted with scene paint and then given a coat of white shellac.

Books

Books are always necessary. They may be made in many ways. The

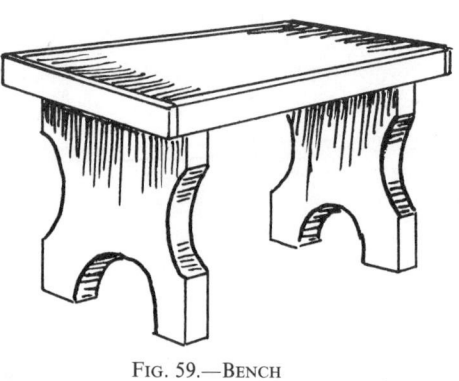

Fig. 59.—Bench

Blocks Screwed to Leg and Rail

Fig. 60.—Table or Chair Construction

backs of old books may be glued to a piece of wall board. Even simpler, simple representations of book backs may be painted on wall board. The upper edge of the board may be cut to show the irregularity in the height of the books. Either way, this type of book strip is attached to a board and set into the book shelf. The strips may be attached to the shelf or remain free. If one book on the shelf must be practical—that is, must be taken out and used—it is very simple to cut the strip of book backs and insert a real book.

Practicals

The term "practical" usually refers to props, but it may refer to almost any object on the stage—door, window, fireplace, etc.—that is actually used. For example, if a door stands open during the entire show it is not practical. If it opens and closes, it is practical. A window that opens and closes is practical. A fire in a fireplace is practical if it is actually burning—that is, lighted with electric lights to make it appear to be burning. A clock that shows the right time, a stairway that is walked on, a lamp that is lighted, a piano that is played—all these are practicals.

Chandeliers, Lamps, Wall Brackets

Chandeliers, lamps, and wall brackets usually are borrowed or

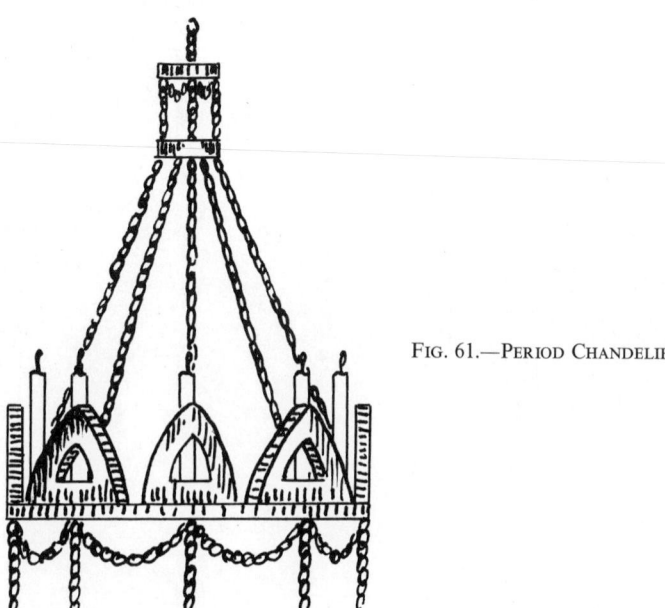

FIG. 61.—PERIOD CHANDELIER

rented. If they are practical they belong to the electrical department; if not, they are props. Frequently it is not possible to borrow chandeliers of the proper type for period plays. An effective, heavy, period chandelier may be made from a ring of wood and a few feet of chain. (See Figure 61.) If it is to be lighted it should be wired with electric candles. If it is not practical, real candles may be used. It is possible, also, to make a fair representation of a crystal chandelier with a light framework of tin. Glass tubing and test tubes may be attached to the frame to give the effect of crystal.

Food

Food is frequently a problem on the stage. For most plays requiring practical food the actual article or a close substitute is best. In some plays, however, the food is primarily for show. For such instances artificial food may be borrowed from stores that use this type of material for display. A small amount of real food may be included with the artificial if some eating is necessary.

Certain foods, such as a roast, a baked ham, and a chicken, may be made simply by sewing cloth bags the general shape of the object desired and stuffing and painting the bags. This method is fast, cheap, and effective.

Papier-mâché

Some types of food and many kinds of props that are hard to find may be made quite easily of papier-mâché. A simple form of papier-mâché is made from shredded newspaper or paper toweling, water, and just enough glue or paste to make the paper cohesive. Objects may be made entirely of paper, or they may be shaped over a form made of wood or wood and poultry wire, window screen, or hardware cloth.

One of the best methods of making papier-mâché objects is to apply papier-mâché over a form modeled of clay or Plasticine. Layers of paper soaked in glue, or wallpaper paste, are laid over the model. The number of layers will depend on the strength required in the finished object. When dry, the object is removed from the model and painted.

Plastics

Plastics are very useful in the making of properties, and a wide variety are available for other stage uses as well. Of the many plastics suitable for stage purposes, perhaps Styrofoam is one of the most versatile. Blue Styrofoam insulation boards from 1 to 4 inches thick are commonly available from suppliers of building and insulation materials, while white boards of smaller dimensions and formed geometric shapes are available at many craft, floral, and decoration supply stores. Either variety may be cut and shaped with common shop tools. Inexpensive hacksaw blades (out of the frame) may be used successfully. Power tools are preferable but will dull rapidly. Unusual shapes and rounded surfaces may be achieved by sanding with a block, an electric disc, or belt sanders. An inexpensive electric hot-wire cutter for cutting and forming the plastic may be purchased from craft shops.

Most common glues may be used for attaching Styrofoam to itself or other surfaces, but water-base glues, such as casein, require a long drying time, and hot-melt glues cannot exceed 165° F, the melting temperature of Styrofoam. (Blue Styrofoam insulation board is fire retardant; white boards and shapes are not.) Styrofoam will dissolve when contacted by the methane and ketone solvents contained in many glues (including styrene cement) and paints. A smooth finish may be achieved on the material by prime coating the surface with latex paint. Any water-base paint may be used for painting Styrofoam; however, all lacquers and many spray paints will dissolve it.

Styrofoam may be used to make lightweight substitutes for heavy objects, such as rocks, or to replace wood, marble, or other types of

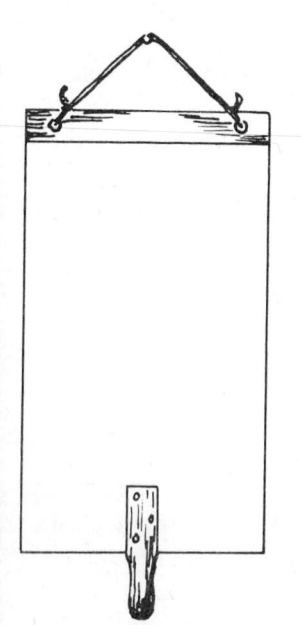

Fig. 62.—Thunder Sheet

ornaments. Cut and assembled, Styrofoam may be used to make moldings, plaques, and panels.

SOUND EFFECTS

Sound effects have undergone a great change in the last few years. Most of the old sound-making devices have given way to sound recordings. The range of recorded sounds is very wide, and the fidelity is very high. Even more important is the fact that a record player or a tape recorder is simpler to operate than most of the old-style effects. In addition, it is easy to buy or borrow sound-effect records and tapes, and it is now quite possible to make special recordings of desired sounds on readily available tape recorders.

If electrical recordings of any kind are used they belong not to the property department but to the electrical department. A few, simple, hand-operated effects classed as props are described below.

Thunder

For thunder a timpani, bass drum, or a thunder sheet—or all three combined—is very effective. A thunder sheet is a large piece of sheet iron, with a rope for hanging the sheet at one end and a handle at the other end. (See Figure 62.) To create the sound of thunder the sheet is vibrated by shaking the handle.

Rain and Waves

A device for creating rain or wave sound effects is equally simple to make. It is an oblong frame of 1 by 3 inch pine, approximately 1 foot wide and 3 feet long, covered on both sides with window screen. A pound or two of peas and beans are placed inside the box. The effect of rain or waves is created by tilting the box. (See Figure 63.)

Wind Machine

A wind machine is a bit more complicated. Two wood discs ap-

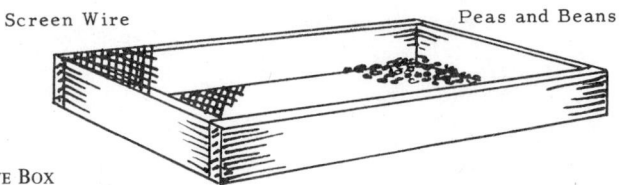

Screen Wire   Peas and Beans

FIG. 63.—RAIN OR WAVE BOX

proximately 18 inches in diameter are held apart by a series of quarter-round strips about 2 feet long. The strips are nailed around the circumference of the discs not over an inch apart. The drum formed by the discs and strips is fitted with a shaft and mounted in a rigid frame, and a handle is attached to one end of the shaft. Next, a piece of canvas is laid over the drum. All but one edge of the canvas is free. This edge is tacked to the base of the framework supporting the drum to hold the canvas in place. When the drum is turned, the friction between the canvas and the quarter-round strips creates a sound similar to that of wind. (See Figure 64.)

Horses' Hooves

Creating the sound of horses' hooves is very simple. All that is needed is a coconut cut in half. The halves are held one in each hand and struck on the floor or on a table.

Bell Box

A bell box is an indispensable prop for ringing door bells or telephone bells. It is a light wood box just large enough to hold two dry-cell batteries of the type used in homes for ringing door bells. Two push buttons, a door bell, and a buzzer are mounted on the outside of the box. One button rings the door bell, the other the buzzer. This arrangement is light, compact, and portable. The bell may also be operated from standard 110V power, but a 6V transformer must be used to reduce the voltage.

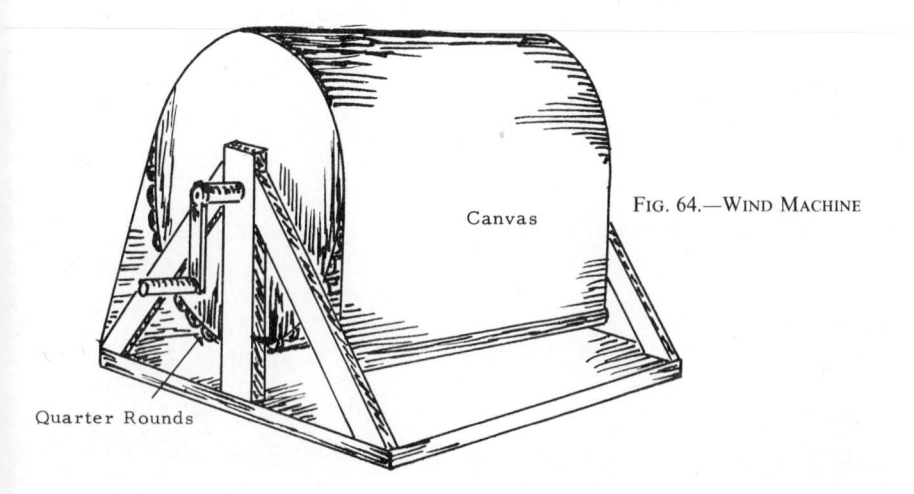

Canvas

Fig. 64.—Wind Machine

Quarter Rounds

8

SCENE PAINTING

Scene painting is sometimes thought of as work for the trained artist. Nothing could be further from the truth. The trained artist frequently lacks the bold approach required for the stage; he produces carefully finished art pieces rather than the bold representations so necessary for the theatre. Art training will prove valuable, of course, but anyone with a reasonable degree of art sense and a large amount of perseverance may become adept at painting scenery. Practice and experience are the important qualifications.

MATERIALS AND EQUIPMENT

Scenery is usually painted with positive dry color (sometimes called "distemper" color): powders in a wide range of colors that are mixed with water and glue to make scene paint. Scenery may also be painted with casein or latex (rubber-base) paint. Oil colors are almost never used.

Dry Colors

The powders from which scene paint is made are available from most theatre supply companies—by the pound—in many colors in their full brilliance, and also in black, white, and a number of browns (earth colors). The colors most commonly used are: light chrome yellow, mineral orange, turkey red lake, American vermilion, purple lake, light chrome green, cobalt blue, ultramarine blue, yellow ochre, raw sienna, burnt sienna, raw umber, burnt umber, Vandyke brown, ivory black, and zinc white. These colors are desirable, but not essential: primrose yellow, medium chrome yellow, bulletin red, magenta lake, emerald green, medium chrome green, malachite green, Italian blue,

81

and Prussian blue. Some of these colors do not mix easily with water, so they are sold in paste as well as in dry form.

Dry color is made into scene paint by using pure colors when strong colors are required; the full intensity or brilliance of the dry color may be changed, if desired, by adding other colors or black or white. Glue and water (dissolved ground sizing glue) must be added when dry colors are mixed for use. The glue is used to bind the powder to the scenery, so an amount sufficient to make the powder adhere is required. If too much glue is added the flat will draw out of shape, and the surface will become very hard and may even crack. Too much glue will also discolor or stain the surface when the flat is repainted. It is difficult to set a rule for the amount of glue required, since the amount varies with the color.

Some dry colors are very light; others are very heavy. That is, the relative weight of the pigments varies according to color. Therefore, the lightweight colors require more glue than the heavy ones. The safest method of determining the amount of glue required is to add a small amount of glue and take a sample and allow it to dry. If the color does not rub off when the sample is dry, there is enough glue in the mixture. If the color does rub off more glue must be added to the mixture. Since too much glue is injurious to the surface of flats, only the smallest amount should be added before the first trial. Experience will make the adding of glue to dry colors a very simple process.

Special colors.—Some dry colors have peculiarities which should be noted. For example, there are two kinds of black: lamp and bone. Lamp black is not suitable for scenery painting. Even bone black is very difficult to mix with water.

To facilitate mixing of bone black, a small amount of dissolved glue is added to the dry powder to form a smooth, thick paste. The paste may then be thinned to the desired consistency. Several other colors should be mixed in this same way; namely, Vandyke brown, reds, gold, and silver.

There are two other methods of handling colors that are reluctant to mix with water. Denatured alcohol may be added to the dry powder; or, an even better method, a small amount of detergent may be added to the dry color and water.

For most scenic purposes gold and silver are mixed with glue, not with bronzing liquid. Gold must be stirred constantly because it settles rapidly; silver must be stirred constantly because it floats on the surface of the water. Both silver and gold require a large amount of glue.

Casein and Rubber-base Paint

Casein paint may be used in place of scene paint. Casein paint is manufactured in paste form, and is, therefore, easy to use. The paste is simply diluted with water and applied. Casein paint is obtainable in white, a wide range of tints suitable for wall decoration, and in all the primary colors. Compared with scene paint, casein has some advantages and disadvantages. When dry, casein is no longer water-soluble; hence it gives a more permanent finish than scene paint. Casein is more opaque than scene paint; consequently it covers old painting more successfully. On the other hand, casein is more expensive than scene paint. Since it is not water-soluble when dry, casein presents more of a problem in the way of keeping brushes, pans, pails, and clothes clean. What has been said of casein is true also of rubber-base paint. It should be noted that casein paints are becoming scarce, as they are being replaced by rubber-base and similar paints.

Colors that Bleed

Reds must be used with care, for they are struck from aniline dyes. It is almost impossible to paint over red. Every time new paint is applied the red dye "bleeds" through and gives the new coat of paint a pink cast. Venetian red is practically the only red which will not "bleed." This color is particularly adaptable for tiled roofs, brick walls, and fireplaces. Occasionally other colors will bleed. Purple is one of them.

If red has been used and it becomes necessary to paint over it, it is advisable to wash off as much of the red as possible. Then if reasonable care is taken in the application of stippling, splatters, and the like, the marks of the red will be quite unnoticeable when the set is completed.

Stirring Paint

All the paints described above are, of course, merely colored pigments suspended in water. It will be remembered that different colors have different densities and settle at different rates of speed in the solution. Consequently, a mixture of several colors must be stirred constantly; otherwise the mixture will change, and it will be impossible to bring it back to the original color because more of one pigment has been used than of another. All paint should be stirred constantly.

Brushes

The brushes used in painting scenery are important. For coating-in, a large priming or calsomine brush 6 to 8 inches wide is used. Priming brushes vary widely in price. A very expensive brush is not necessary, but acceptable work cannot be done with a cheap one. Nylon brushes are very good.

For detailed painting, lining, and so forth, it is necessary to have a variety of small brushes ranging from ¼ inch to 2½ inches in width. These brushes should be long-handled, stiff-bristled brushes, like those used by artists. They, also, vary in price according to the width of the brush and the length of the bristles. If long-handled brushes are not available, oval sash brushes can be used.

In addition to priming and long-handled brushes, the scene painter should have two or three ordinary brushes varying in width from 3 to 5 inches. They are particularly adaptable for painting woodwork and graining scenery. A long-handled feather duster is needed for feather-dusting painting, and coarse sponges for stippling.

Mixing Equipment

For mixing paint one should have three or four medium-size galvanized pails and at least a half-dozen cheap tin pans or Number Ten cans. A granite pan with a dipper-like handle is desirable for preparing glue if an electric glue cooker is not available.

If boiling water is not readily obtainable, some provision should be made for a gas ring or an electric plate for heating water and for dissolving glue. If glue is boiled or heated on a stove, it must be done in a double boiler; otherwise the glue will stick to the bottom of the pan and burn.

There are a few other incidental items essential to painting. They are, in order of their importance, a straightedge or lattice strip at least 6 feet long, a yardstick, chalk, charcoal, and a chalk line.

STEPS IN PAINTING A SET

The steps to be followed in painting a set are:

1. Wash the flats if necessary. Washing may be done before or after the flats have been battened together.

2. Give the new flats a coat of paint if they are to be used with old flats in the same set. If all the flats are new this step is unnecessary.

3. Patch any holes there may be in the flats.

4. Strip, or Dutchman, cracks between flats that are battened or hinged together.

5. Give the set one thin coat of paint.

6. Apply the final coat of paint.

7. Decorate the surface as desired.

8. Paint the woodwork. Woodwork that is to be handled is sometimes painted with casein or rubber-base paint for greater permanence. Woodwork may also be painted with scene paint and then given a coat of clear shellac for permanence and for a low gloss ffnish.

9. Touch up when the set is in place.

Washing Scenery

Flats may be repainted almost indefinitely, but if the paint on them becomes too thick it will crack or chip off. The remedy for chipped or cracked paint varies with the condition of the flat. If the frame is in good condition but the cloth is torn, patched, and loose, the frame may be re-covered. If, however, both frame and cloth are good, the flat may be washed.

The method of washing may vary with the facilities for washing. The essential materials consist of plenty of warm water and a large, coarse sponge. The water must be used freely, but care should be taken to avoid soaking the cloth loose from the frame or water-soaking the keystones and corners. It is unnecessary to wash off all the paint. The flat should be wiped free of all excess water before it is allowed to dry in order to avoid runs and streaks which leave water stains that are difficult to paint over.

Patching

Torn cloth may be patched very easily, from either the front or the back of the flat. A piece of unbleached muslin somewhat larger than the hole is painted with the same paint that is to be used for painting the set. Then the area around the hole is painted. The painted side of the patch is placed against the torn flat, paint to paint, and the whole patch is painted again and allowed to dry.

Dutchmaning

A Dutchman is a strip of unbleached muslin used to cover the cracks between flats that are battened or hinged together. The strip should be about 4 inches wide—wider if it must cover hinges—long enough to reach from top to bottom of the flat. A number of short pieces may be used.

The process of applying a Dutchman is similar to that of applying a patch. The strip is painted, and the area on either side of the crack is painted. The strip is then placed over the crack, paint to paint, painted again, and allowed to dry. The flats should not be folded while the Dutchman is wet. Strips should not be set flush with the top and bottom of the flat but, rather, about ½ inch short on each end. Care should be taken in both Dutchmaning and patching to avoid wrinkles in the cloth and to keep the edges smooth and securely stuck. This procedure makes for a smooth, unbroken wall surface and eliminates cracks between flats. Cloth should not be dipped into the paint, as wrinkles result and cannot be removed.

Coating-in Scenery

New cloth may or may not be sized. Sizing is not a special process involving special materials. It is merely the first coat of scene paint or dry color. It serves to fill the pores of the cloth and to remove the slack and wrinkles by shrinking the muslin. It is possible to put only one coat of paint on a flat and to proceed immediately with decoration. However, the surface will be more satisfactory for decoration if more than one coat of paint is applied.

When old and new flats are combined in a set it is advisable to paint all the flats one color—about the tone desired for the finished set. Then the final coat may be applied. When new and old scenery is being coated-in, the new scenery should be painted first. Then the paint should be thinned for the old scenery. The more paint there is on the old scenery the more necessary it is to thin the paint. Old paint absorbs more water than new cloth.

In order to know exactly how thin to mix the paint for any particular work, it is well to experiment by applying some of the mixture to the corner of a flat. If the brush seems to stick or hold to the scenery, the paint is not thin enough. The brush should slip easily and smoothly over the surface of the work. On the other hand, if the paint has a tendency to run on the surface of the work, it is too thin.

When flats are being coated-in care should be taken not to brush back over a surface that has just been painted. The water softens the undercoats, and brushing back causes the underpaint to mix with the new paint. Furthermore, paint should never be applied evenly in one direction but, rather, should be brushed on lightly in all directions, and no attempt should be made to smooth away brush marks with parallel strokes. The surest way to cause a streaked appearance is by trying to prevent it.

Decorating the Set

Some form of surface decoration is necessary to break the flat and uninteresting surface of the painted scenery. Surface decoration also affords an opportunity to introduce more color and texture into the set. It may be done in several ways.

Stippling.—Stippling is used to represent tiffanied walls, old or rough stone, plaster, and some types of wallpaper. The colors used vary with the effect desired. If stippling is done to give color and tone to a wall of a room, the colors most commonly used are light yellow, light blue, and pink. It is very important that the colors be applied evenly to avoid spotty, blotch effects. All colors used should be of the same tone or intensity, so that no one color will dominate the others.

To insure an even stipple, one person should do all the stippling of one color, for no two people stipple exactly alike. (This is generally true of all texturing techniques.) Also, only one sponge should be used for each color because no two sponges produce the same effect. In fact, to insure the best results one person should stipple the entire set with one sponge. That, however, is not always essential.

Spattering.—The spattered effect is obtained by dipping the brush into the color to be applied, wiping it carefully across the edge of the pail to remove the excess paint from the bristles, and shaking it at the flat with a snapping motion of the wrist. The particles of paint fly from the brush and spread themselves evenly over the surface of the flat. Spattering may be done also by drawing a knife or a sharp-edged stick over the bristles of the brush, causing spots of paint to spatter on the scenery, or by holding the brush in one hand and striking the heel of the brush against the fist of the other hand.

Spattering is effective for general wall toning, and it is especially valuable for toning or aging scenery that is painted to represent old stone, wood, or plaster. Both spattering and stippling require practice, if they are to be done well.

Feather-dusting.—Another interesting over-all texture may be obtained by dipping a feather duster into paint, bouncing the duster a time or two on a surface such as a piece of cardboard, plywood, or wax paper to spread the feathers, and then bouncing the duster with a twisting motion on the flat, which is placed face up on the floor. Colors used are the same as in other texturing techniques.

Dragging.—Dragging, or dry-brushing, is done by, first, dipping the brush into the paint and wiping it very dry. This causes the bristles to separate and stand apart in clusters. Then this dry brush is dragged over the flat. This technique produces the effect of the grain of wood or the rough trowel marks in plaster.

Dragging to represent graining in wood is usually done with three shades of one color. If, for example, the base color is a medium tan, a light tan is first dragged over this body color. Then a tone darker than the base is applied in the same manner. A small brush may be used to add additional graining accents, high lights, and shadows. Paint may be lightened with any color except white. Likewise, paint may be darkened with any color except black. White makes colors appear chalky; black deadens them.

The same principle of three tones of the same color is used for rough, troweled plaster effects. However, to achieve plaster effects, short, curved strokes are used in painting, instead of the long strokes used in achieving graining effects. Practice alone will perfect these techniques.

WALLPAPER EFFECTS

A figured texture representing wallpaper is essential for some types of stage sets. Scenery is never papered but is painted to look like paper. For the wallpaper effect the set is stencilled with a large wallpaper design.

If stencil paper is not available an excellent substitute is tagboard —a material similar to manila letter folders. Tagboard must be coated on both sides with shellac, lacquer, varnish, or tung oil to make it waterproof. The design is traced on the paper and cut out with a sharp knife or razor. The pattern is then stencilled onto the set with a reasonably dry brush. Care must be taken to have the paint thick enough so that it will not run under the stencil. To insure that the stencils are properly applied, the entire set is marked off in rectangles and one pattern stencilled in each area.

Other simple wallpaper effects may be obtained with the use of patterned rollers or with rollers to which pieces of sponge have been attached. Roller patterns may be combined with stripes painted at intervals to divide the roller patterns.

PANELLING

If a set is panelled, the strip around the panel is usually the color of the rest of the woodwork. This strip, or molding, varies in width according to the style of the panel. To give the panel molding the effect of three dimensions high lights and shadows are added. The color of the high lights and shadows depends of course on the color of the woodwork. For example, high lights on cream may be blue, light yellow, or white. Shadows then will be light tan or light lavender. High lights on brown may be yellow, light tan, or blue-gray. Shadows then will be dark blue, dark brown, or purple.

The location of lights and shadows is fairly simple to determine. It must first be decided from which side the light is supposed to come. If, for example, light is from the right, the right edge of each panel molding will be in light and the left edge will be in shadow.

The source of light is usually from a window, which is above the bottom panel molding and below the top panel molding. The light then will be at the top of the lower panel molding and at the bottom of the upper molding. It follows that the shadow in this situation will be at the bottom of the lower panel molding and at the top of the upper panel molding.

If the source of light is in the center of the set it will be necessary in some instances to have the light and shadow arrangement different on both sides of the set. However, in most instances, particularly for stock scenery, the actual source of light need not be taken into

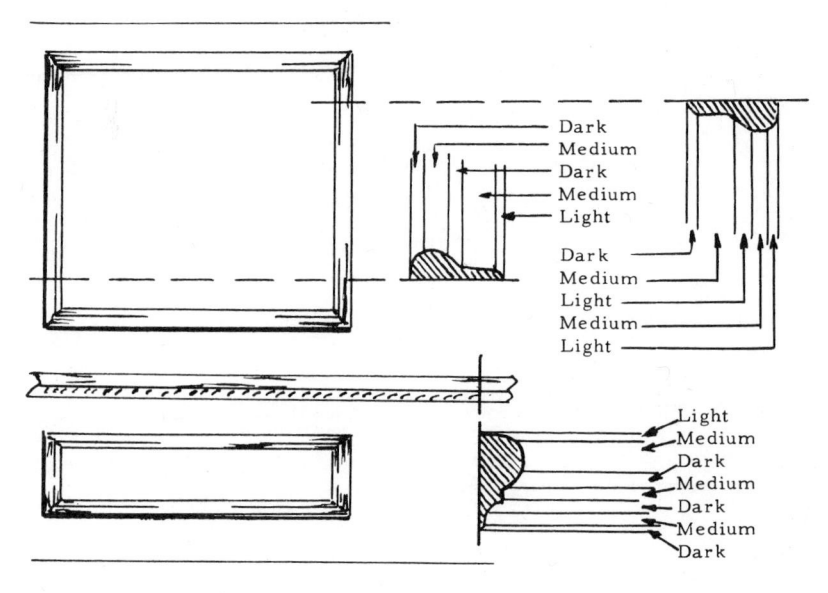

FIG. 65.—HIGH LIGHTS AND SHADOWS IN A PANELLED SET

consideration. (See Figure 65.) More elaborate panels are merely a further development of the same principles of light and shadow. Light and shadow must be used also to develop form in baseboards and picture moldings. This may be done with a few or with many lines, depending upon the effect desired.

SIMPLE INTERIORS

Flats used as interiors are usually divided vertically into three parts: (1) the baseboard, or mopboard, (2) the wall proper, and (3) the drop ceiling. The baseboard is usually about 12 inches wide, but for some types of sets it may be from 30 inches to 4 feet wide, and it is called a dado. The wall may run to the top of the flat, but it usually stops 1 to 2 feet short of the top of the flat. At this point a picture molding is frequently used. If the wall does not run to the top of the flat the third division is the drop ceiling, which varies in width according to the height or design of the set.

The baseboard should match the doors and windows. They may vary in color from cream to dark brown. The walls may be any color, but for most purposes tan will be found to be very practical. The picture molding should match the woodwork. The drop ceiling is usually cream or light tan. It is a general rule that all colors used for stage purposes must be slightly darker or brighter than those regu-

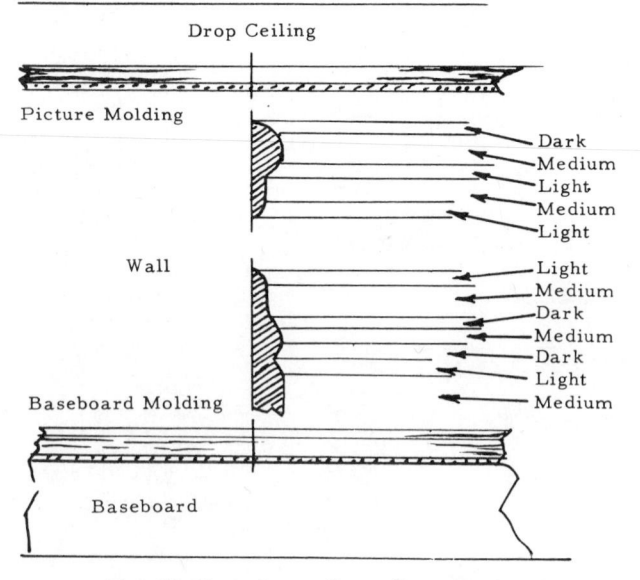

FIG. 66.—PAINTING THE SIMPLE INTERIOR

larly used for interior decoration because light tends to make colors appear light or faded. (See Figure 66.)

Scenery surfaces are treated not only to give variety and patterns to the flats but also to introduce as many colors as possible into the set. The more colors introduced into a surface, the greater are the possibilities of lighting, for light must have color to fall upon if it is to help create the illusion of texture and solidity.

PROBLEMS IN PAINTING

Some problems in painting may be solved by observing actual objects. For example, if bricks are to be painted for a wall or a fireplace it is advisable to study their actual size, shape, arrangement, and color. Also, it may be helpful to study pictures of objects to be painted to see how artists have simplified their subjects and how they have secured the effect of shape, perspective, light, and shadow.

Enlarging

Occasionally it may be necessary to paint a backdrop or some other piece of scenery by enlarging an original sketch or picture. Enlarging may be done very simply by the squaring method shown in Figure 67. The picture or sketch is divided into a number of small

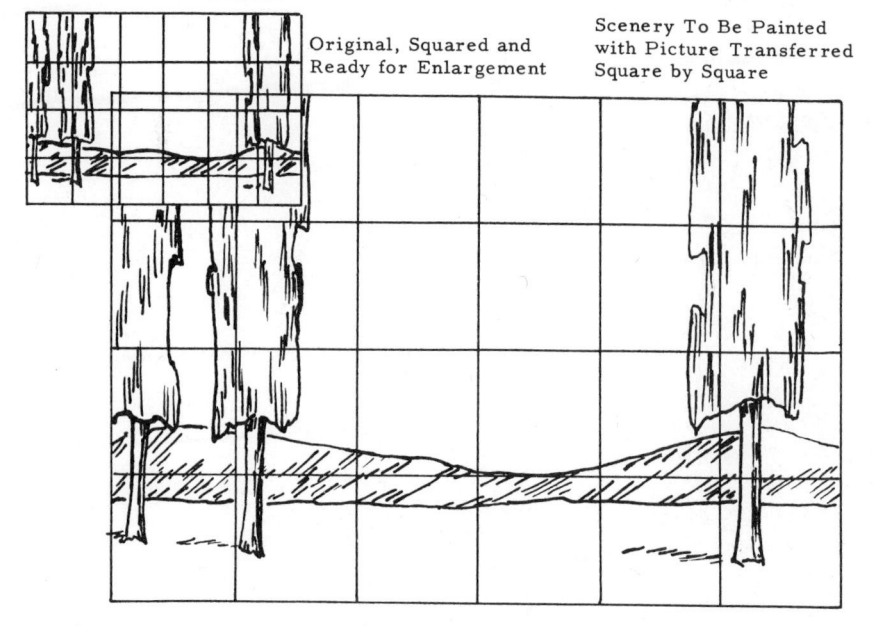

FIG. 67.—ENLARGING FROM A SKETCH

squares, the surface to be painted is divided into the same number of large squares, and the drawing is transferred, square by square, easily and accurately.

COLOR THEORY

There are other, more complicated color theories, but this very simple one will serve. There are three primary colors from which all other colors are made: red, yellow, and blue. There are also three secondary colors: orange, made by combining red and yellow; green, made by combining yellow and blue; and purple, made by combining red and blue. (See Figure 68.) Red, yellow, and blue mixed in equal proportions should give gray or black but usually give some form of brown because of unequal mixing or pigment impurities.

This simple color theory applies to pigments which are reasonably pure. Unfortunately, it does not always apply to the colors used in scene painting, since the cheap colors used here do not always produce the colors desired. Whenever possible it is advisable to buy a wide variety of colors rather than to attempt extensive color mixing. (Standard colors most commonly used are yellow ocher, raw sienna, burnt sienna, raw umber, burnt umber, Vandyke brown, ultramarine blue, chrome yellow, chrome orange, chrome green, vermilion, black, and white).

EFFECT OF LIGHT ON COLOR

It is necessary to consider colors not only as they affect each other

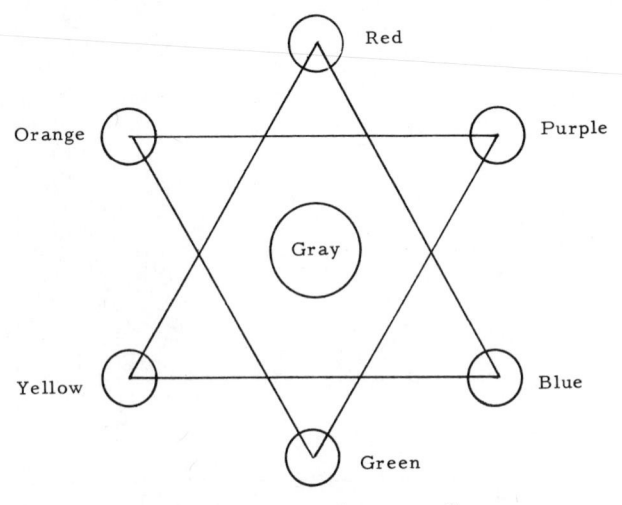

FIG. 68.—PRIMARY AND SECONDARY COLORS

but also as they are affected by light. In general it is true that the addition of any color of light has the same effect as the addition of a pigment of the same color. For example, a blue light on a yellow surface will tend to turn the surface green. However, few definite rules can be given because of the impurities in both pigment and light.

In the laboratory accurate results can be achieved from mixing pigment and light, but it is difficult to achieve the same results under the less ideal conditions of the stage. However, in spite of the uncertainties of the stage, a few results of mixing pigment and color are certain. If the light is the same as the color upon which it falls it will intensify that color. If, however, the light is the opposite or complement of the color upon which it falls—for example, red light on green, orange on blue, yellow on purple, or vice versa—the light will tend to turn the color to black.

Color and lighting are discussed further in the following chapter on stage lighting. The few facts given above will serve as an aid and a guide in painting scenery. The most important elements in successful painting are, as has been stated before, practice and experience.

9

STAGE LIGHTING

Electricity was not in common use on the stage until about 1900, and it was another ten or fifteen years before adequate controls were developed. Many of the electrical devices in use in the theatre are of even more recent development. In fact, it might be said that stage lighting with electricity is the only new feature in any of the theatre arts.

When the control of electricity was perfected and high intensity lamps developed, the theatre at last had light in abundance, after centuries of semidarkness. The natural result was an overabundance of lighting. If a little light was good, more was considered better. The stage was flooded with light from every possible angle. The settings were illuminated until they appeared flat. Depth and solidity were lost as a result of the absence of shadows. Every nook and corner was as brightly illuminated as the center of the stage.

Light and shadow are the factors that make for visibility. One is seen by contrast with the other. When a light wipes out shadows, visibility goes with the shadows. Consequently, overillumination of the stage also affected the appearance of the actors. They were so completely flooded with light that their very features were blotted out, and in order to be seen at all actors were forced to resort to all manner of make-up. Strong footlights killed the natural shadows around the eyes and caused other shadows, if they caused any at all, to appear opposite to those which are caused naturally by sunlight. In order to appear more nearly human, actors painted in shadows with grease paint. Make-up is of course still used, but it is used to accentuate the shadows made by more natural illumination on the stage.

As a reaction to overillumination there has been a tendency on the part of some producers to underlight. This is equally objectionable. Light should be considered in its relation to the production and not as an independent medium to be used either for mere illumination or for the creation of artistic effects independent of the play itself.

Light and color have the power to depress or exhilarate, both in nature and on the stage. Stage lighting, properly used, seeks to make use of this power of light. Light is an important factor in helping the director create the desired effect. Not only is the audience affected, but the actors also respond to light, and the same illumination which creates atmosphere for the audience also aids the actors in entering into the mood of the play.

No attempt will be made here to present an elaborate discussion of lighting and stage wiring. However, a few simple fundamentals are essential to give information to those who may not be interested in an exhaustive study of lighting but who have elementary lighting problems which may be solved by simple, brief explanation. It is also possible to obtain valuable information from the catalogs of companies that manufacture stage lighting equipment.

WATTAGE, AMPERAGE, AND VOLTAGE

In any discussion of lighting it is essential to consider three common terms used in connection with electricity. They are wattage, amperage, and voltage. Voltage is reasonably constant, but amperage varies according to the number of lights that are burning on any one circuit. For this reason it is necessary to know the principles of amperage, wattage, and voltage and to understand how they are used in determining line load, because variable load factors determine the sizes of wires, cables, cable connections, and fuses. All electrical equipment is rated according to its amperage capacity. For example, fuses are rated as 5, 10, 15 amps and so on.

In discussing electricity it may be necessary to point out for the benefit of the uninitiated that there are two types of current: alternating and direct. Direct current (DC) flows constantly in one direction. Alternating current (AC) flows alternately in one direction and then in the other. This change in direction, known as a cycle, occurs 60 times a second. Most current in the United States is 60 cycle AC.

Voltage

Voltage is the force with which the electric current flows through a wire. The voltage in the average electrical service is 110, usually written 110V. Voltage may vary slightly, but slight variation is not significant to stage uses. The main reason why voltage is of interest in this discussion of stage lighting is that voltage is important in determining amperage. Occasionally voltage may be found to be less than or more than the standard 110V. If voltage is very low, equipment will not function properly. If voltage is too high, equipment may burn out. A 110V lamp at 55V will burn half-bright; at 220V it will burn out in a matter of minutes.

The wires that bring electricity to the stage are usually referred to as "service." Normally three wires are run to a switchboard or to a company box. (A company box is a switch box on the stage to which a portable board may be connected.) The center line is known as the common negative, or ground. The two outside lines are positive. If lines are run from the center line and one of the outside lines the two lines will be 110V. If the outside, or positive, service lines are extended they will be 220V. The two outside lines are not usually used in this way. The arrangement of three wires is used to give greater service with less wiring. (See Figure 69.)

Wattage

All lamps and dimmers are rated in watts. Wattage is a measure of the amount of electricity that is consumed in a given length of time. The amount of light that a lamp gives may also be indicated in watts. This rating is stamped on the end, or base, of every lamp. When more than one light is burning on any one cable or group of cables coming from one source of electric current the wattage of the individual lights is added to give the total wattage of that circuit.

Amperage

Amperage is the speed or flow of current through a wire. This flow creates heat. In general, the greater the speed, the greater the heat

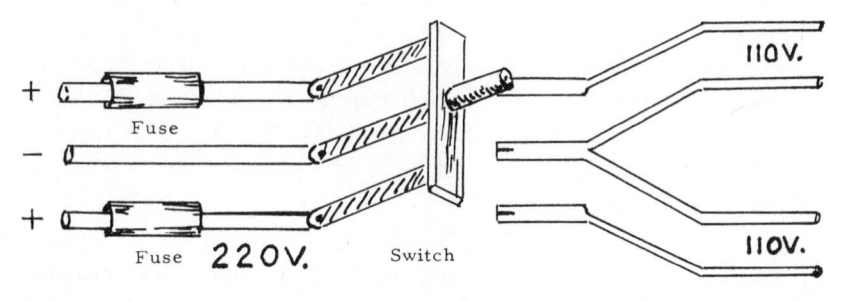

FIG. 69.—DIVIDING 220V

produced. Given the wattage and voltage, it is a very simple matter to calculate the approximate amperage of any light circuit. The formula is $W \div V = A$, where W is the wattage, V the voltage, and A the amperage.

Amperage is an important consideration in determining the size of cables, connections, and fuses. Improperly calculated amperage may not only cause fuses to blow but may also result in overloading cables to the point where the heat generated causes the cable to burn. The formula given above simply means that with a load of 1,000 watts at 110V a 10 amp fuse is needed; 2,000 watts of light will require a 20 amp fuse. The greater the size of the light, the greater is the speed of electric flow required to supply that light, and the more heat produced.

USING ELECTRICITY

Fuses

A fuse is a protective device inserted in an electric line. It is designed to melt at a low temperature and thus break the electric circuit in case the line is overloaded or in case there is a defect in equipment or wiring. A blown fuse is a sign that something is wrong. The trouble should be found and eliminated before a new fuse is installed. Replacing a fuse with a new one the same or larger size without locating the cause of the trouble is not a solution, because the fuse will continue to blow until the cause of the trouble is eliminated.

Cable and Wire

Size.—Like fuses, cables and wires are made to carry a certain amperage load. The size of the wire is specified by number—for example, 16, 14, 12, 10. The larger the number, the smaller the wire. Number 14 cable is the size most commonly used for general stage purposes. For some purposes a much heavier cable is necessary. The amperage capacity of commonly used cable sizes is as follows:

16	14	12	10	cable size
6	15	20	25	amperage capacity

Types of cable.—Either stage cable or rubber covered cable should always be used on the stage. Rubber covered cable is more flexible and, though more expensive, more durable than stage cable. Under no circumstance should ordinary lamp cord be used. It is not heavily enough insulated for stage use. Cable is walked on constantly, and scenery is dragged around with no thought of the wires that may be on the floor. If for no other reason, lamp cord should not be used because it does not pass the inspection of fire insurance underwriters, and its use may result in cancellation of fire insurance.

Care of cable.—All cable should be carefully coiled and put away when not in use. Cable should not be cut unless absolutely necessary, and rented or borrowed cable should never be cut.

Connectors

If at all possible, special stage connectors should be used. They are fireproof and almost indestructible. There are two types of stage connectors: stage receptacles and plugs; and slip, or pin, connectors.

A stage receptacle is an oblong porcelain box open at the ends. On two inside edges there are copper plates, which carry the current. Stage receptacles are placed in stage pockets—metal boxes built into the stage floor or wall. Two or more receptacles are usually placed in each pocket. A stage plug is an oblong fiber block with copper plates on two opposite sides. Stage cables are attached to the copper plates with large screws. The connection is formed when the stage plug is placed in the stage receptacle. (See Figure 70.)

Slip, or pin, connectors are attached to the ends of cables and to lighting equipment. They are used to connect a cable to a light or to connect two cables. Slip connectors are made in three commonly-used sizes: 5 amps, 15 amps, and 30 amps. The different sizes cannot be interplugged. (See Figure 71.) Many electrical codes require a third, or ground, wire on electrical equipment, as a safety factor.

Plugging Box

One other item of importance is the plugging box, which is used when it is necessary to use more leads of cable than the floor pockets

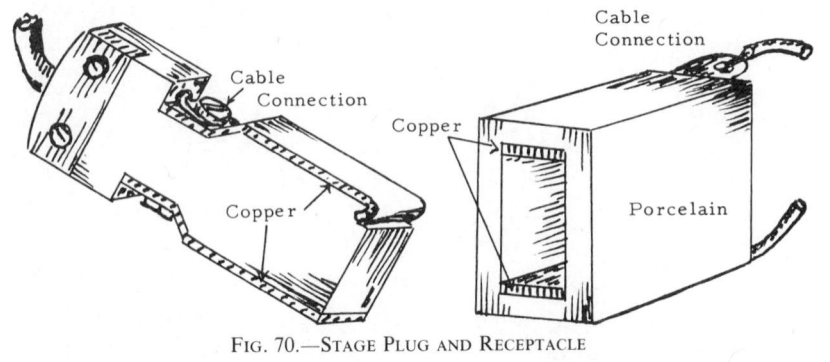

FIG. 70.—STAGE PLUG AND RECEPTACLE

permit. A plugging box is a heavily constructed box of wood and iron with four or more stage receptacles in the sides or ends. (See Figure 72.) The box is connected by a heavy cable to a stage pocket. By using a plugging box it is possible to get many leads from one pocket, but care should be taken to prevent overloading the pocket to which the plugging box is attached.

Lighting the Production

There are two methods of lighting any production. One is general illumination, and the other is specific illumination. The primary purpose of general illumination is visibility; specific illumination, as the term implies, is for lighting particular areas on the stage. This adds a dramatic or artistic quality to the lighting.

General Illumination

The most common sources of general illumination are footlights, border lights, and floodlights. General illumination is intended to distribute light evenly over the entire stage. The color and intensity of the light may be varied, but there is very little control over the area lighted. All objects, important or unimportant, are lighted equally, and everything on the stage is seen as though it were of equal importance.

General illumination usually indicates too much light, but it is possible to have over-all illumination of such low intensity that visibility is lost. It is always important that the audience be able to see. There seems to be a correlation between seeing and hearing, and what an audience does not see it often thinks it does not hear.

One particularly important function of general illumination is the lighting of the sky cyc. In most instances a sky requires a very even

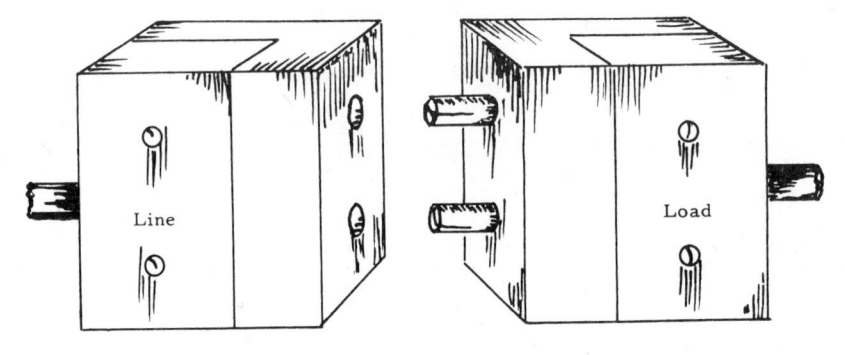

Fig. 71.—Slip or Pin Connector

light; if there is any change or blend of color it is very gradual. Lighting the cyc may be done with the upstage border, but if the cyc requires light on the sides as well as at the back a series of hanging floodlights must be used up and down stage. Floodlights may be placed around the base of the cyc on the floor back of a ground row. Light from both top and bottom is almost necessary. An ideal arrangement for cyc lighting is a special horseshoe-shaped border at the top of the cyc with a series of similar lights for the floor. The floor lights should be made in sections so that they may be removed when not in use.

Specific Illumination

Specific lighting is designed to light a particular area or series of areas on the stage. This type of lighting is done with spotlights because they are so mounted and constructed that their light beams can be directed to specific locations, and the size and shape of the area lighted can be controlled. Specific lighting does for a stage what a painter does for a canvas. A painter accentuates what to him seems important and minimizes what seem to him unimportant details. A spotlight focuses attention on an important area and in that way minimizes the importance of the rest of the set. Such lighting creates a center of interest and increases pictorial and dramatic effect. Specific lighting also tends to unify a stage picture.

Specific lighting may overaccentuate action areas, just as general lighting may flatten out the stage picture by a lack of accent. If action areas only are lighted, or if they are overlighted, it is possible that actors moving from one place to another may have to pass through unlighted areas. Footlights and border lights are very useful in eliminating these dark spots. In fact, that is the greatest service that foot-

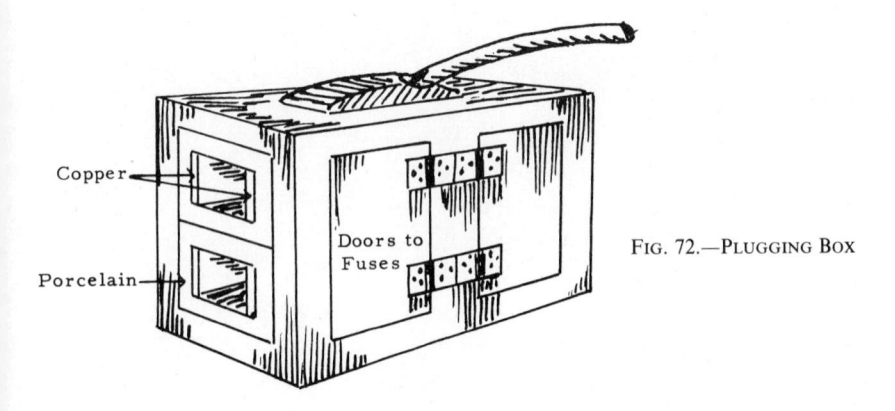

Copper

Porcelain

Doors to
Fuses

FIG. 72.—PLUGGING BOX

lights and border lights render. By judicious use of footlights and border lights the spots of light created by spotlights may be blended to form an even, yet interesting, stage picture.

LIGHT CONTROLS

The success of either general or specific illumination depends entirely on the proper control of lighting instruments. The controls may be divided into six categories as follows: (1) the control of turning lights off and on (one of the functions of the switchboard); (2) the control of dimming lights (the other function of the switchboard); (3) the control of direction of lights (accomplished by the way they are mounted or hung); (4) the control of the size of the spot of light (through the lens or housing around the lamp); (5) the control of the shape of the spot of light (by shutters); (6) the control of the color of light (with colored lamps or filters).

The Switchboard

The switchboard, which controls all lights, is located on one side of the stage or in a booth at the rear of the auditorium. Each electrical outlet, circuit, or series of outlets on the stage comes to switches on the board. The switchboard may be simple or complex, depending upon how completely it controls the stage lighting instruments. Ideally, every instrument should have a separate switch, and these switches, in turn, should be controlled by master switches so that any light may be turned on and off independently or in conjunction with any other light. In addition the switchboard should have adequate control of the intensity of the light. Beside switches for turning lights on and off there must be dimmers. Several circuits may be sent through one dimmer, but, ideally, every circuit should have a separate dimmer.

The switchboard need not be elaborate. A board of a simple type for a small stage may have no more than ten or twelve dimmers. In such a board, probably three dimmers would be used for footlights, if there are any, three for borders, and the rest for either floor pockets or spotlights. In addition to the circuits on dimmers there may be any number of circuits or outlets without dimmers. Ideally, however, every circuit should have a dimmer.

Since there are many types of boards, all working differently, and since the more complicated switchboards must be factory built, it would be impractical to describe their construction and operation.

However, a simple portable board which may be made locally is described below. Boards with the same characteristics may also be purchased as a prefabricated package.

The portable switchboard.—A portable board may be much smaller than a permanent board, because it is flexible and has no connections that are permanent. All lights are connected temporarily to the board by stage cable with slip connectors or stage plugs. The board itself is connected to the company box. Portable boards vary greatly in size. The size is limited by the weight of the board. If it is too large and too heavy it will be difficult to move about easily.

As few as four dimmers may be used effectively for simple productions. With four dimmers, each dimmer should be attached to two receptacles. There may be two or more receptacles on the board without dimmer control. These receptacles are said to be "hot." Such an arrangement makes possible the burning of lights that may not need dimmers. (See Figure 73.) Individual lights may be controlled by breaking the cable connections at the board or by giving each receptacle a control switch. The latter is a more desirable arrangement, but it is not absolutely essential for a simple portable board. However, a small board is practical only if every circuit is interchangeable and if all parts are working at all times.

The wiring diagram shown in Figure 73 illustrates the usual practice of supplying 220V to the board and dividing it into 110V circuits. The common wire runs to all outlets. Half of the outlets are supplied by one side of the 220V line, the other half from the other side.

Dimming Lights

Resistance dimmer.—At one time, the most commonly used dimmer was a resistance coil, or rheostat. This dimmer consumes electricity instead of allowing it to go to the lamp, and it works equally well on AC and DC. The light intensity is regulated by a sliding handle which governs the amount of current consumed by the dimmer. As the handle turns in one direction, resistance is increased and the light goes out; as the handle turns in the other direction, resistance is decreased and the light comes on. Controls may be designed to slide up and down, instead of around.

The size of the resistance dimmer used in a switchboard is very important, because the dimmer and light load must balance. Any size, or capacity, dimmer will not dim any size load. Dimmers are rated in watts, and the rating is stamped on them. In order to know when a dimmer is properly loaded, the wattage of all lights on the circuit is added. The wattage of the lights should be equal to, or approximately equal to, the wattage rating of the dimmer.

A resistance dimmer is inserted into one side of the line and wired in series with the lights to be dimmed. The electricity that should make the lamp filaments glow is given off by the dimmer as heat. If too many lights burn on one dimmer, the dimmer will become overheated and burn out. On the other hand, if the load is too small, the light will not dim out entirely. Occasionally a small light—a spotlight or part of a border, for example—must be dimmed on stage when no small dimmer is available. In such an instance, a light large enough to balance the load is added to the circuit off stage. Then the on-stage light will dim with the one off stage. This off-stage light is called a phantom load.

Autotransformer dimmer.—Because of its greater efficiency, this dimmer has superseded the resistance dimmer. Instead of consuming electricity, the autotransformer dimmer reduces the voltage supplied to the light. Since only the current used by the light is consumed, electricity is saved. Transformer dimmers are wired into both lines, in parallel with the lights to be dimmed. The dimmer and the load need not be balanced. Any size lamp may be dimmed. Overload should of course be avoided. Autotransformer dimmers operate on AC only.

Tube dimmer.—A third type of dimmer is the vacuum, or thyrotron, tube dimmer. It is entirely electronic and can be remotely controlled,

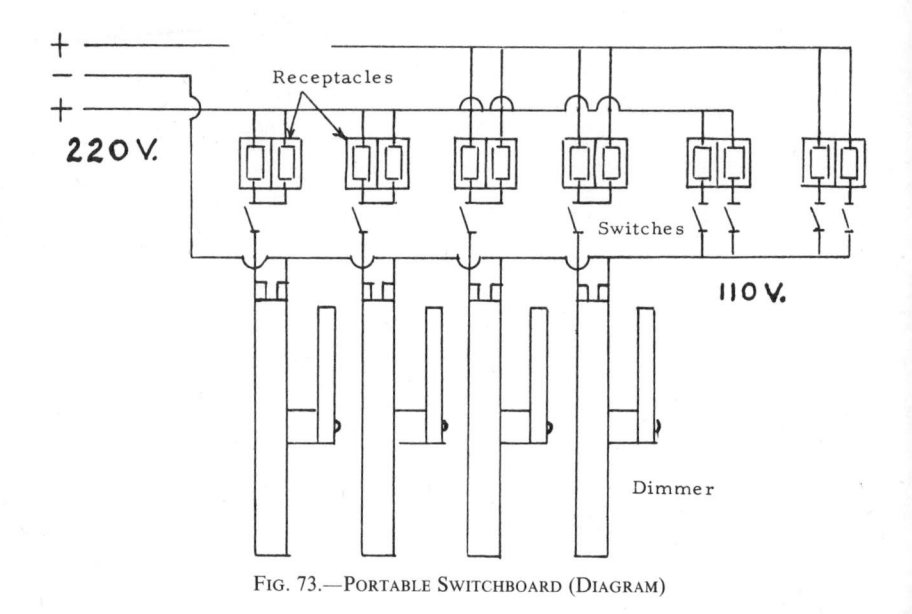

FIG. 73.—PORTABLE SWITCHBOARD (DIAGRAM)

making it unnecessary to use valuable stage space for bulky, awkward dimmers. This dimmer is now seldom used, as solid state components have replaced tubes in a new type of control.

Silicon controlled rectifier dimmer.—A more recent dimmer development makes use of silicon rectifiers. This control combines all the advantages of other types of dimmers with that of being relatively small and light in weight. This system allows the dimmers to be remotely located, with the controls almost anywhere. It is also possible to preset light cues and move easily and rapidly from scene to scene.

Direction of Light

The direction of light is controlled in several ways. Footlights may frequently be tipped at various angles to throw light either up or straight back on the stage. Border lights may be tipped on their battens to light straight down, downstage, or upstage. These are relatively crude directional controls.

More accurate are the universal joint type of adjustment on light stands for lights on the stage floor and yokes and batten clamps for instruments that are hung. The lights are supported in such a way that they can be raised and lowered, twisted from side to side, or

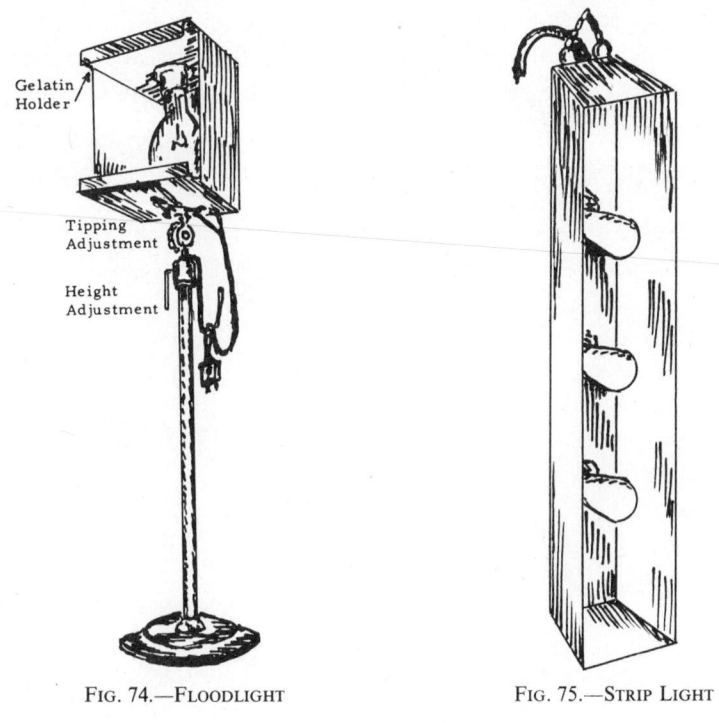

Gelatin Holder

Tipping Adjustment

Height Adjustment

FIG. 74.—FLOODLIGHT   FIG. 75.—STRIP LIGHT

tipped up and down. These joints and clamps make possible highly accurate direction of any beam of light.

The three major types of lighting instruments that are primarily directional are footlights, border lights, and floodlights.

Footlights.—Footlights are located at the front edge of the stage apron.

Border lights.—Border lights are hung so that they may be raised and lowered. The first border should be on the second set of lines back of the working curtain or the portal. The second border light is 6 to 8 feet upstage of the first border, and so on back for each succeeding border light.

Floodlights.—Floodlights are also called bunch lights and olivettes. They are of box-shaped construction with one open side. The flood is equipped with a very large, or mogul, socket suitable for a 1,000 watt lamp. At the top and bottom edges of the open side there is a groove to support a wood frame which holds a sheet of colored gelatin. (See Figure 74.) Floodlights are of two general styles. One style is equipped for attachment to a standard for use on the floor to light doorways, drops, cycs, etc. The other style is designed to hang above the set to light action areas, a backdrop, or a cyc.

Strip lights.—Though of minor importance compared with foots and borders, strip lights are also directional. They consist of one to four small lights in an open reflector, frequently a tin pan. (See Figure 75.) Strip lights are used to light doorways.

Size of the Spot of Light

Regardless of their design, all spotlights operate on the same principle. An intense light is confined in a metal box. The light can leave only through a round opening in one end. As it passes through this opening the light is further controlled by a lens which regulates the size of the beam of light. Therefore, most spotlights cast a concentrated light on a small area. The size of this spot of light can be definitely controlled by the lens or by the position of the lamp in the metal box. (See Figure 76.)

The lens.—The spotlight lens, or condenser, is a circular glass, flat on one side and convex on the other. The flat side of the lens is placed toward the light. The degree of convexity of the other side regulates the size of the light beam. A slightly convex lens causes the light rays to widen rapidly and cast a large spot. This kind of lens is called a wide-angle lens. A highly convex lens, called a long-focus lens, causes the rays of light to widen slowly and cast a very small circle of light. The flat-convex, or plano-convex, lens casts a hard-edged light.

Plano-convex lenses in spotlights have been almost entirely superseded by a special type of lens known as a Fresnel. It is not used principally for the control of the size of the spot of light; that is done by moving the lamp in its metal box. The advantages of the Fresnel over the plano-convex lens is that the Fresnel is designed to transmit more light and to give a soft-edged light. This lens has one smooth surface. The other surface is ribbed or stepped. (See Figure 77.) The Fresnel lens is now so widely used that the instruments using them are referred to as Fresnels.

Lamp position.—Although major changes in the size of the spot of light are made through changes of lenses, minor changes can be made by moving the lamp within the instrument. The spotlight lamp socket is attached to a sliding base. The lamp may be moved forward or backward. As the lamp is moved away from the lens the spot of light becomes smaller; as it is moved toward the lens the spot of light becomes larger. (See Figure 76.)

Shape of the Spot of Light

The control of the shape of the spot of light is accomplished with

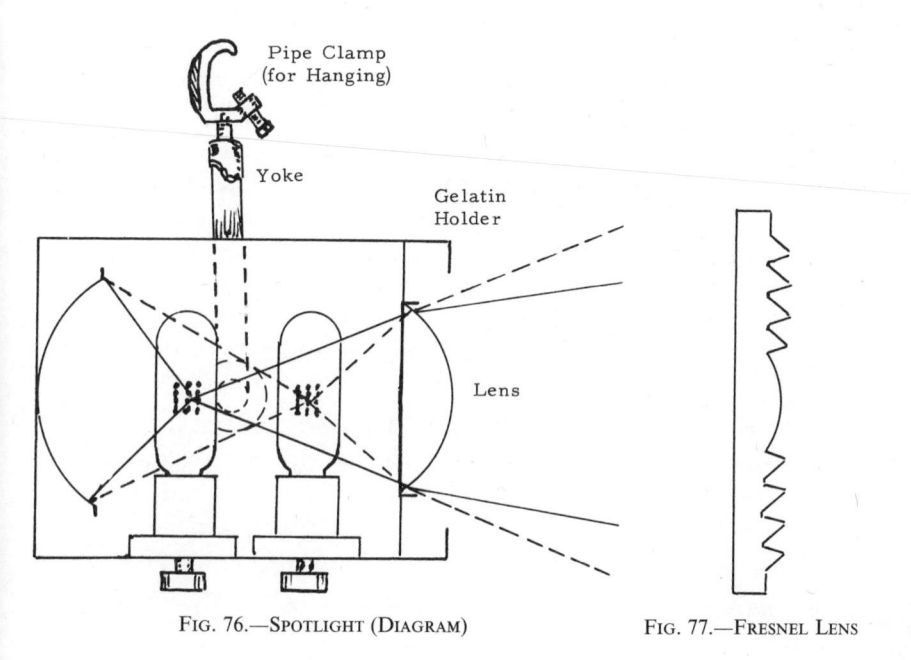

Pipe Clamp
(for Hanging)

Yoke

Gelatin
Holder

Lens

FIG. 76.—SPOTLIGHT (DIAGRAM)   FIG. 77.—FRESNEL LENS

some form of shutter. Spotlights are built with shutters already attached, or they may have shutters attached to them. Shutters are simply four strips of metal mounted over the front of the light so that they may be moved in or out over the front of the spotlight to cut off any portion of the spot or regulate the shape of the spot. Temporary shutters, frequently called barn doors, are attached to a groove on the front of the spotlight.

More efficient than shutters attached to the front of the spotlight are those built as an integral internal part of the lamp house. An example of this kind of spotlight is the ellipsoidal spotlight, which is used when it is necessary to control accurately the shape of the spot of light. The entire construction of the ellipsoidal spotlight differs from an ordinary spotlight. The lamp is inserted upside down into an ellipsoidal reflector located at the rear of the instrument. The light filament is in the exact focal center of the mirror. The light rays are gathered and projected to an aperture which acts as a shaping device. The mirror in this instrument greatly increases light output. Four swivel shutters, located at the aperture, may be moved in or out or be tipped to create the shape desired. The shape of the spot is projected through the lens onto the stage. The lens is adjustable to control the focus of the projected spot of light. (See Figure 78.) Ellipsoidal spotlights may also be built with an iris.

All spotlights are available in a variety of sizes. The sizes commonly used on the stage range from 250 or 500 watt baby spots to 1,000 or even 2,000 watt spotlights. Some spotlights are illuminated with carbon arc lights. This type of light is used when the light must be very brilliant and when the distance from the spotlight to the stage is very great. Arcs are not often used in nonprofessional productions.

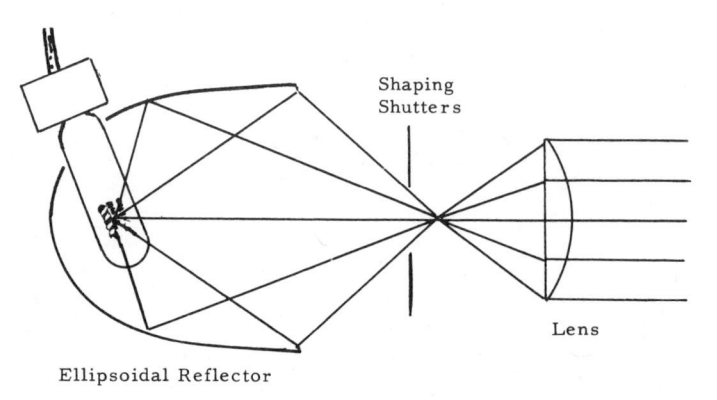

Shaping Shutters

Lens

Ellipsoidal Reflector

FIG. 78.—ELLIPSOIDAL SPOTLIGHT (DIAGRAM)

Most spotlights are equipped with prefocussed sockets or bases. With this type of socket the lamp is not screwed in but is inserted in a fixed position. The fixed position guarantees that the filament, the mirror, and the lens will be aligned properly for greater light output. Spotlights with plano-convex and Fresnel lenses frequently are equipped with concave mirrors mounted directly back of the lamp to increase the illumination.

Quartz Iodine Lamps

Quartz iodine, or tungsten halogen, lamps have a great advantage over standard condensed filament tungsten lamps. Because they are smaller, they are made of quartz rather than glass to withstand great heat. Although they are more expensive, they have a life of up to 2,000 hours; and the inside of the envelope never turns black, so the light output never changes. These lamps will fit most existing instruments, but some instruments are designed especially for quartz.

The Color of Light

The color of light from all lighting instruments is controlled with colored glass, gelatin, or plastic. Each of these color mediums has its advantages and disadvantages. A limited variety of colored lamps are also available.

Glass.—The advantage of glass is that the colors are permanent, nonfading. Also, glass is usually of such thickness and quality that breakage is very rare. Disadvantages include expense and limited color range available in glass. Glass is most adaptable to footlights and border lights.

Gelatin.—Gelatin comes in tissue paper-thin sheets. It may be obtained in as many as a hundred different tints and shades. The advantages of gelatin are the wide variety of colors and the very low

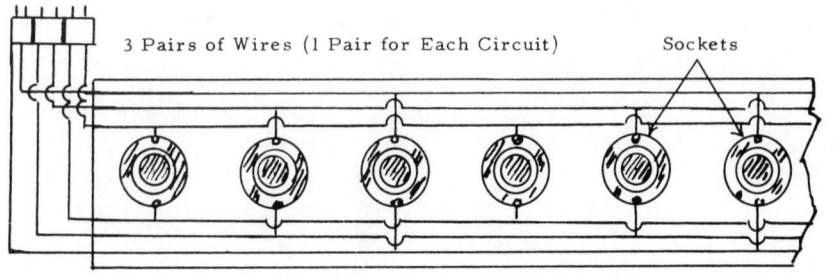

FIG. 79.—WIRING FOR SIMPLE FOOTS AND BORDERS

cost of the medium. However, gelatin colors fade, and the sheets are easily cracked, torn, or broken.

Plastic.—Plastic is similar to gelatin, but heavier, more durable, and moistureproof. It is also more expensive, fades as badly, and is limited in color range.

Color Illumination

Footlights and border lights are the principal sources of color illumination. The simplest form of foots and borders is a trough with a series of colored lamps. (See Figure 79.) The other type of foots and borders is much more satisfactory. In this type each light is confined in a separate open-faced compartment. The light in each compartment is colored by colored glass or by a colored gelatin screen placed over the open side. (See Figure 80.)

Footlights and border lights should be a series of lights in alternating colors separately controlled, so that any one color may be used independently of any other color. The colors in foots and borders are usually red, blue, and green. Amber and white are sometimes added.

PROPER USE OF LIGHTING INSTRUMENTS

For best possible results lighting instruments should be properly placed and properly used. Floodlights should be used for general backstage illumination to illuminate backdrops and cycs, to throw light through windows, to give light from the wings in an outdoor set, and in some few instances to light doorways. Floodlights should be kept as high as possible and tipped down to avoid undesirable shadows.

Footlights should be used with care. They should always be the least important source of light. They should never be so bright that they cast shadows on the back wall.

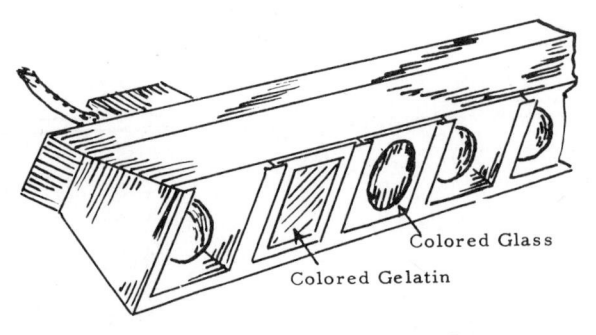

FIG. 80.—COMPARTMENT-TYPE FOOTS AND BORDERS

Strip lights should be used in all doorways; otherwise the opening is dark and the effect of entrances and exits is spoiled. There are special cases, of course, in which the script requires that the adjoining room be dark. Generally, however, openings are lighted.

The first border light should be hung as far downstage as possible directly in back of the first spot batten; otherwise actors may be in the dark if they work downstage, or, what is nearly as bad, they may be lighted by the footlights alone. In sets with ceilings, only the first spotlight batten and the first border are used. The light should be kept subdued as much as possible and still be effective. Too much border light becomes glaring and disturbing.

Uses of Spotlights

The location of spotlights for stage illumination varies with the specific lighting problems to which they are assigned. Spots are located directly back of the grand drapery or portal, and may be augmented by the first border light. The first spot pipe, or batten, in all cases should be hung directly in front of the first border light. The number of spots in this position is governed by two factors: the amount of space available across the opening and the number of spots that may be bought, borrowed, or rented.

Spotlights in the first border position are used to illuminate the important acting areas in the following manner: the spotlight farthest to the left illuminates the right center of the stage; the spotlight at left center illuminates extreme stage right; the spotlight on right center illuminates extreme left, etc. In this way, instead of coming directly down on the stage the rays of the lights strike the faces of the actors at an angle. Seldom, if ever, are they focussed straight down. This principle of lighting at an angle holds true in general for the setting of all spotlights.

Spotlights used from the back of the auditorium, from the auditorium ceiling, or from the balcony rail should be handled the same as spots from the first border. They should be cross-focussed. They may be focussed on definite playing areas or used to flood the stage. If such spots are used it may be possible to eliminate the footlights. In addition, spots may be used from the side of the stage for the effect of sun or moon through windows and for lighting halls or stairways. They should be raised as high as possible, and the light should be focussed down through the opening to avoid undesirable shadows.

Proscenium or tormentor spots.—Spots may be mounted on each side of the stage just back of the proscenium or the tormentor. In this position they are particularly useful for lighting the downstage right and left corners. The spotlights are attached to a vertical batten. Lights and batten in this position are called a boomerang. Additional boomerangs frequently are used farther up stage for side lighting. They may also be moved off the stage into the side aisles of the auditorium. This is particularly advantageous if the production is moved out onto the apron in a semi-thrust arrangement. Many auditoriums have slots built into the side walls to facilitate this type of lighting.

Balcony spots.—It is difficult to light the faces of actors playing downstage. For this reason, balcony spotlighting has been developed. A series of spots is placed just below the balcony railing or in a beam in the ceiling of the auditorium. The spots usually are set to cover the downstage acting area, and the lights are placed with care to avoid shadows on the back wall of the set. If shadows do occur they may be eliminated by readjusting the spots or by increasing the intensity of light on the stage to offset the shadows cast by the balcony spots. Light from spotlights mounted in this position is not always distributed evenly over the entire stage but is focussed so that the greatest amount of light is centered on the stage locations where the most important action takes place.

If the setting is very open, backlighting may be effective. The instruments are hung high and far upstage, pointing downstage. This lights the backs of the actors and the scenery, creating a three-dimensional effect.

Special effects.—Spotlights are used also for special effects such as sunlight or moonlight through a window, for illumination of stairways and hallways, and, in some instances, for casting shadows required for special dramatic effects. Shadows should never be eliminated but should be controlled and used in such a way that they aid in creating the stage picture.

Colored light, as well as shadow, may be used to create remarkable atmospheric effects, either realistic or abstract. There is no better way to create an effect of sunlight in a room than to use a yellow or amber light in such a way as to cast light and shadow on the floor or opposite wall. The same is true of moonlight. The stage may be dimly lighted with blue light coming through a window or door. It is the contrast of light and shadow aided by color that creates the desired effect.

Lighting for theatre-in-the-round and thrust staging.—This lighting is not very different in principle from proscenium productions. The instruments more completely surround the action, with the audience also surrounding the stage. Care must be taken in the placement of lights to prevent the light from crossing the stage and lighting the audience on the other side. This is usually accomplished by mounting the instruments relatively high.

Natural Source of Light

As far as possible a set should appear to be lighted by a natural source of light, unless the production is intended to be unrealistic. A day scene in a room should seem to be lighted through windows with floodlights or spotlights. When artificial light is the obvious source for an evening scene, table and floor lamps, wall brackets, and chandeliers are used. They supply the apparent source of light, but this apparent source of light is augmented by concentrated light from spotlights overhead which cover the same areas.

If, for example, a table lamp is being used in a scene the lamp should be lighted with a very small light. This light has very little effect on the lighting of the stage. In order to make the lamp appear to give as much light as it does in a room a spotlight must be set to cover the same area that the table lamp itself illuminates.

Care must be taken to eliminate unnecessary light. This does not mean under-illumination; it means that every scene has a point to which it should be lighted. That point is not the same for any two scenes but varies according to the mood and the time of the action. If too much light is used perspective and aesthetic distance are destroyed. Unnecessary light is distracting to the audience and is tiring to the eyes. Whenever possible direct light should be kept off the scenery.

PROJECTED EFFECTS

The word "effect" has another meaning in connection with stage lighting. Effects are round, flat metal boxes, inside of which are discs which are rotated by clockwork. The discs are transparent. They are painted to represent clouds, fire, water ripples, snow, and the like. The effects are attached to spotlights, and the particular representation painted on the disc is projected onto drops of various kinds to create the effect of moving clouds, sparkling water, leaping flames, falling snow, etc. In front of the effect is an effect, or objective, lens; the lens makes it possible to focus the effect at various distances. In addition to the more common effects, there is a large variety of novelty effects, such as moving landscape, waving flag, climbing monkey, electric fountain, lightning zigzag, flying fish, and so forth. Effects are expensive to buy, but they may be rented from any stage lighting company for a nominal fee.

Another form of projected scenery is achieved without the use of lenses. Opaque, or translucent colored, masks are placed in front of a powerful light similar to a floodlight. This throws a dark or colored shadow onto a surface. These masks may take many forms—trees, housetops, abstract shapes, anything. This method is called "Linneback" projection. Scenery may also be projected with slides from a standard slide projector.

THE EFFECT OF LIGHT

Light, particularly colored light, always effects a change in the appearance of a surface upon which it falls. The result is not always the color cast on the surface. For example, a red surface becomes a deeper red under a red light but nearly black under a green light. The way in which light changes the color of objects on the stage presents a major problem, especially since the times when light may be used to change color are few, while the times when light changes color when it should not be changed are many.

Color Mixing

Mixing colored pigment and colored light presents three problems: (1) mixing of pigment with pigment, (2) mixing of pigment with colored light, and (3) mixing of colored light with colored light. When the three primary colors of pigment—red, yellow, and blue—are combined in equal proportions and are seen under white light the combination will appear gray or black. When the three primary colors of light—red, green, and blue-violet—are combined in equal proportions the result is white light. When colored light and colored pigment are mixed, the result is usually the same as that of mixing two pigments. For example, when red and green pigment are combined they form gray or black. Red light on a green surface will make the surface appear gray or black. Blue and yellow pigment form green. Blue light on a yellow surface turns that surface green.

All the hues of the spectrum may be obtained by changing the proportions in mixing either pigment or light or both. The results and the success in mixing, however, will be determined by the purity of the pigments or light colors combined.

In view of the above facts it is obvious that the color of each object on the stage should be considered in terms of the color of light to be used, and vice versa. When scenery is painted the artist should know what lights are to be used for the setting, or he should be the one to decide on the color of lights for the setting and work accordingly.

Color on Make-up and Costumes

The generalizations on color mixing apply to costumes and make-up. Colors which can best be used without affecting make-up are rose pink, light lavender, chocolate, light scarlet, and amber. The first two colors are very flattering. Blue and green usually have just the opposite effect. They will turn make-up black and spotty. One shade of blue can be used without seriously affecting make-up—steel blue.

All materials are affected by colored light; silks are especially susceptible. A change in the color of the light will completely change the color of the costume. Frequently, bright costumes are changed to muddy-looking rags because of improper lighting. On the other hand, costumes may be improved by light. Because of the differences in the way materials and colors react to each other, trial and error in lighting is as important in obtaining effect as following elaborate rules.

THE LIGHT PLOT

Quite as important as the equipment in lighting a production is the light plot with its light cues. Every production should have at least one light rehearsal, and before this rehearsal a light plot with its cues should be prepared. The light plot is a diagram of the stage showing the position of all lights. (See Figure 81.) The cues are the signals for turning the lights off and on.

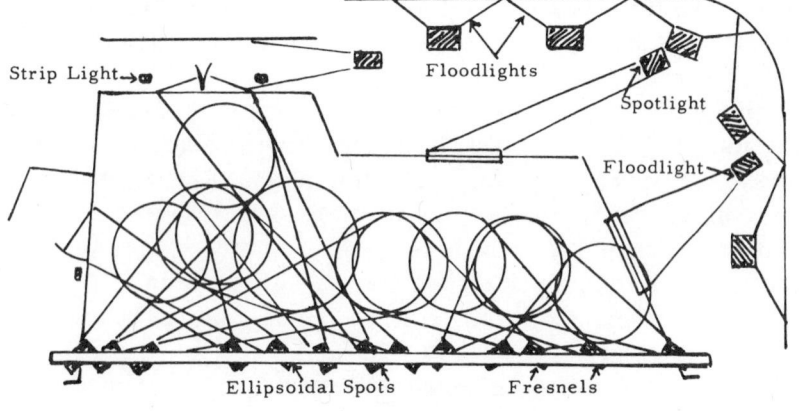

FIG. 81.—LIGHT PLOT

At the light rehearsal all the lights should be tried out and rearranged if necessary. The cues should be worked over carefully with the actors, the director, the electricians, and the stage manager so that the moment the actor gives the cue the electrician makes the necessary light changes. Many performances are ruined because there was not a careful light rehearsal.

BIRDSEYE LAMPS

If the spotlights, floodlights, strip lights, border lights, and footlights described above are not available, or if quick additional lighting equipment is needed, there is a simple, inexpensive substitute. It is the R 40 or PAR 38 lamp, commonly known as Birdseye lamp. This lamp does not take the place of regular stage equipment, but it is a boon to people without equipment and a wonderful auxiliary source to those who have equipment.

Birdseye lamps are somewhat bell-shaped. They are mirrored in the back. They project a beam of light straight forward. They are made in two styles: a flood lamp, which is generally directional, and a spot lamp, which concentrates the light in a relatively small area. They are also made in a number of different wattages: 75, 100, 150, and 300 watts. The R 40 is designed primarily for indoor and protected use; the PAR 38 is made of heavy cast glass and will withstand rough treatment and may be used outdoors in all weather.

An almost endless variety of fittings may be bought to add to the usefulness of the Birdseye lamps, such as sockets that may be swiveled in all directions, metal rings to hold color filters, and spill rings to further control the light rays.

In addition to their use for specific illumination, Birdseye lamps may be used to advantage in border lights in place of regular lamps. Here it is possible to decrease wattage and increase illumination.

WITH LIGHTING, as with designing, building, and painting scenery, nothing takes the place of practice, perseverance, and experience in creating effects that take their proper place in the artistic whole of a dramatic production.

GLOSSARY OF STAGE TERMS · INDEX

GLOSSARY OF STAGE TERMS

ACT CURTAIN—The curtain at the front of the stage; also called *working curtain*. Used to open and close each act; may be used between scenes.

ASBESTOS CURTAIN—A fireproof curtain which drops and seals the proscenium opening in case of fire on the stage; also called *the asbestos*. *See also* Fusable Links.

ASTRAGAL—A molding used as a doorstop on one of double doors.

AUTOTRANSFORMER DIMMER—A type of dimmer which controls light intensity by changing the voltage in the circuit.

BABY SPOT—A small spotlight of 250 to 500 watts.

BACKDROP—One or more large pieces of cloth hung at the back of the stage as the back of a set. Also called *drop*.

BACKFLAP HINGE—A hinge with two square blades by which it is fastened.

BATTEN—A piece of 1 by 3 inch lumber used to build scenery, to fasten scenery together, and to suspend scenery. *Also* a pipe from which scenery is hung.

BIRDSEYE LAMPS—Bell-shaped lamps which project beams of light straight forward. Used for auxiliary lighting or in place of floods and spots.

BOARD FOOT—A piece of lumber 1 foot long, 1 foot wide, and 1 inch thick; the unit of measurement in purchasing lumber.

BOOMERANG—Vertical pipe at the side of the stage holding spotlights for side lighting.

BORDERS—Cloth hung from side to side of the stage to mask the top of the set. *Also* strips of lights hung from side to side of the stage above the set.

BOX SET—A set made up of flats enclosing the acting area. Usually used to represent a room or an interior scene.

BRACE—*See* Stage Brace.

119

Brace Cleat—A metal plate attached to a flat, into which a stage brace is hooked. Also called *stage brace cleat*.

Bunch Light—*See* Floodlight.

Butt Hinge—A hinge with two oblong blades by which it is fastened.

Carpenter, Master—*See* Master Carpenter.

Casein Paint—Prepared water paint to which casein glue has been added.

Casing—The frame around a door opening.

Ceiling—A frame covered with cloth, painted, and placed on top of a set to represent a ceiling.

Ceiling Irons—Metal plates with rings; used to hold pieces of the ceiling frame together and to attach lines supporting the ceiling above the set.

Circuit—The lights or electrical outlets controlled by one fuse.

Clear—The order given by the stage manager to the cast or crew to leave the set area.

Clinching Iron—A piece of boiler plate about 10 inches square; used for clinching nails.

Clout Nail—A wedge-shaped soft iron nail; used in building scenery.

Condenser—A plano-convex lens; used in spotlights.

Corners or Triangles—Right angle triangles of quarter-inch plywood; used in building scenery.

Counterweight System—The arrangement of battens, lines, and weights used in raising and lowering scenery.

Curtain Line—The place where a curtain, usually the act curtain, touches the stage floor.

Cut-down Set—A form of box set, usually not more than ten feet high, set inside a cyc or legs and backdrop. Also called *vignette*.

Cyclorama—Cloth hung to enclose the acting area. Also called *cyc*.

Dimmers—Mechanical or electronic devices for controlling the intensity of lights. *See also* Autotransformer Dimmer; Resistance Dimmer; Thyrotron.

Distemper Colors—Dry powdered pigment used in making scene paint.

Door Iron—*See* Foot Iron.

Door Stop—A molding attached to a door jamb to keep the door from swinging through the opening.

Dragging—A painting technique employing a partially dry brush.

DROP—*See* Backdrop.

DROP CEILING—A light-colored band, usually cream, painted around the top of a box set.

DRY COLOR—Colored powder from which scene paint is made.

DUTCHMAN—Cloth used to cover cracks between flats in a set.

DUVETYN—An inexpensive cotton cloth with a soft flannel texture on one side.

EFFECTS—Mechanical devices attached to spotlights for projecting on scenery images such as clouds, rain, snow, etc. The lens used to focus an effect on scenery is called an *effect lens* or *objective lens*.

ELECTRICIAN, MASTER—*See* Master Electrician.

ELLIPSOIDAL SPOTLIGHT—A spotlight equipped with an ellipsoidal mirror for greater light output and shutters to control the shape of the light.

FALSE PROSCENIUM—A proscenium inside the permanent proscenium which can be changed to fit a particular play. Also called *portal*.

FEATHER DUSTING—A painting technique using a feather duster.

FIRE CURTAIN—*See* Asbestos Curtain.

FLATS—Wood frames covered with cloth and painted.

FLIES—The area above the stage. Also called the *fly loft*.

FLOODLIGHT—An open-faced metal box on a stand housing a large light, usually 1,000 watts. Also called *bunch light* and *olivette*. Used for general lighting.

FLOOR PLAN—A plan or drawing showing the location of scenery as it rests on the stage floor.

FLY LOFT—*See* Flies.

FLYMAN—The stagehand who raises and lowers scenery attached to a set of lines.

FOOT IRON—A band of iron used to strengthen the bottom of a door flat; sometimes called *door iron*. *Also* a piece of stage hardware used to fasten scenery to the stage floor.

FOOTLIGHTS—A strip of lights across the front of the stage. Usually recessed into the stage floor.

FRESNEL—A spotlight using a fresnel, or ribbed lens.

FULL STAGE—The entire acting area of the stage.

FUSABLE LINKS—Small metal links which melt at a relatively low temperature; used in the counterweight system of the asbestos curtain. *See also* Asbestos Curtain.

GELATIN—A tissue-thin sheet of gelatin placed in front of a light to change its color.

GRAINING—A painting technique done with a relatively dry brush to simulate the grain of wood.

GRAND, OR GRAND DRAPERY—The border at the top of the proscenium opening just back of the asbestos curtain. Sometimes used to control the height of the proscenium opening.

GRIDIRON, OR GRID—The iron framework above the stage in which the rigging for raising and lowering scenery is located.

GRIPS—Stagehands who move the scenery.

GROMMET—A metal eyelet or reinforcement for a small opening in the top of cloth scenery; used for lashing scenery to battens.

GROUND CLOTH—A heavy canvas covering for the floor of the acting area of the stage.

GROUND ROW—A piece of scenery, usually a wall, a distant hill, etc., placed in front of a cyclorama or a backdrop.

GUILLOTINE CURTAIN—A curtain that raises and lowers.

HANGING IRON—A metal plate with a ring. Used for attaching lines to scenery for raising and lowering the set.

HARDWARE CLOTH—A coarse metal screen; used in constructing set pieces, such as trees.

HEAD BLOCK—A multiple pulley or sheave over which lines pass from the grid as they drop down to the pin rail.

HORIZANT—A permanent quarter of a sphere used to represent a sky. Also called *plaster dome; sky dome.*

IRIS—A mechanical device attached to the front of a spotlight to increase or decrease the size of the spot of light.

JACK—A triangular brace for scenery; constructed from 1 by 3 inch lumber.

JOG—A narrow flat, usually 1 to 4 feet wide.

KEYSTONE—A piece of quarter-inch plywood cut in the shape of a keystone; used in building scenery.

LASH CLEAT—Any piece of stage hardware around which a lashline may be hooked; used in holding scenery together.

LASHING—The process of fastening two pieces of scenery together with a lashline.

LASHLINE—A length of cotton rope or line used for fastening two flats together.

LEGS—Pieces of cloth 6 to 12 feet wide and of varying lengths hung off and on stage. Usually hung in pairs on stage left and right.

LOAD—The number of lights or pieces of electrical equipment supplied by one circuit. *Also* the combined load on all circuits.

LOCK RAIL—The device which secures the lines used to raise and lower counterweights. *See also* Pin Rail.

LOFT—*See* Flies.

LOFT BLOCKS—Sheaves or pulleys over which lines pass for raising and lowering scenery.

LONG-FOCUS LENS—A lens which creates a small spot of light at a long distance.

LONG LINE—The line of a set of lines that goes to the floor on the side of the stage opposite the pin rail or lock rail.

LOOSE-PIN BACKFLAP HINGE—A backflap hinge with a removable pin holding the two blades together.

MASK—To set or hang scenery in such a way as to prevent the audience from seeing backstage or above the set; for example, placing a piece of scenery back of a door or a border above the set.

MASTER CARPENTER—The stagehand in charge of all scenery and of the scenery crew.

MASTER ELECTRICIAN—The stagehand in charge of all lights and of the electrical crew.

MASTER PROPERTY MAN—The stagehand in charge of all properties and of the property crew.

MOGUL SOCKET—A larger than standard size socket; used with a very powerful light, such as a 1,000 watt light.

MUSLIN—Unbleached cotton cloth used to cover flats.

NOSE—The portion of a step tread which projects beyond the step riser.

NOSE AND COVE MOLDING—Molding combining the nose of a step and the cove molding normally attached to the rise of the step under the nose. Also called *overhang*.

OBJECTIVE LENS—*See* Effects.

OFF AND ON STAGE—Parallel to the footlights.

OLIVETTE—*See* Floodlight.

OLIO—A curtain directly back of the teaser and tormentor.

OPERA DRAPE—A curtain which is draped up on each side of the center to form the stage opening.

OPERATORS—The stagehands who operate electrical equipment.

OVERHANG—*See* Nose.

PAPIER-MÂCHÉ—Paper and paste mixed together; used to model such objects as rocks, fruit, masks, etc.

PARALLEL—The framework made of 1 by 3 inch lumber to support a platform.

PIN OR SLIP CONNECTOR—A piece of electrical equipment designed to connect two cables.

PIN RAIL—The railing at one side of the stage to which lines used to raise and lower scenery are tied. *See also* Lock Rail.

PIN—Object of metal or wood to which lines are tied on the pin rail. *Also* the wire holding together the two blades of a hinge.

PHANTOM LOAD—A light burned off stage in order to load a resistance dimmer to its full capacity.

PLACES—The order given by the stage manager for the cast and crew to stand by for the beginning of an act or for a scene shift.

PLASTER DOME—*See* Horizant.

PLATFORM—The top, or cover, for a parallel; used to raise action or pieces of scenery above the stage level.

PLUGGING BOX—A box with several stage receptacles supplied by a single cable; used to increase the number of available electrical outlets.

PORTAL—*See* False Proscenium.

PRACTICAL—The term applied to any stage property or object used by the actors during the play—furniture that is sat on, rocks that are walked on, food that is eaten, windows that are opened and closed, etc.

PROFILE—The irregular edge of a piece of scenery constructed to represent rocks, trees, etc.

PROJECTED EFFECTS—*See* Effects.

PROPERTY MAN, MASTER—*See* Master Property Man.

PROPERTIES—Anything used or handled by actors during the play.

PROPS—Abbreviations for properties. *Also* the nickname for stagehands who handle properties.

PROSCENIUM ARCH—The opening between the stage area and the seating area through which the play is viewed.

PROSCENIUM SPOTS—Spotlights located on either side of the proscenium opening.

PULL-OFF RIGGING—The line used to open and close a traveller curtain.

RECEPTACLE—Electrical outlet into which a stage plug is fitted; housed in a stage pocket, usually in the stage floor.

REP—A heavy, ribbed cotton material; sometimes used for making cycloramas.

RESISTANCE DIMMER—A mechanical electrical device which controls the flow of electricity to lights by consuming part of the current.

RETURNS—Two pieces of scenery set left and right off and on stage just back of the proscenium opening to mask the downstage edge of the set.

SASH CORD—A braided cotton line used in lashing pieces of scenery together.

SCENE PAINT—Usually a mixture of colored powder, glue, and water to form a substance that may be applied to scenery.

SELVAGE—The heavy, nonfraying edge on each side of a length of cloth.

SET OF LINES—Three lines in the same plane running from the stage floor to the grid and then across and down to the pin rail. Used to raise and lower scenery.

SET PIECES—Miscellaneous pieces of scenery such as rocks, walls, trees, house exteriors, distant hills, etc.

SHEAVES—Wheels or pulleys over which lines pass.

SHUTTER—A mechanical device attached to the front of a spotlight to control the spread of light.

SILICON CONTROLLED RECTIFIER DIMMER—An electronic dimmer using silicon rectifier.

SKY CYC—Cloth, usually blue, enclosing the entire stage area. Used to represent a sky.

SLIP CONNECTOR—*See* Pin or Slip Connector.

SPATTERING—A painting technique used to create texture and add color to a set.

SPECIFIC ILLUMINATION—The lighting of a particular area on the stage.

SPOTLIGHT—A metal box housing a highly concentrated light, with an opening on one side covered by a lens. May be hung from a batten or mounted on a stand. Used for specific illumination.

STAGE BRACE—A piece of stage hardware adjustable in length; used to support scenery.

STAGE BRACE CLEAT—*See* Brace Cleat.

STAGE CREW—The entire production staff of a play.

STAGE MANAGER—The person in charge of all backstage operations during a production.

STAGE PEG—Stage hardware used to fasten stage braces to the stage floor. Also called *stage screw.*

STAGE POCKET—The housing for the stage receptacle; usually located in the stage floor.

STAGE PLUG—The electrical connection which fits into the stage receptacle.

STAGE SCREW—*See* Stage Peg.

STIPPLING—A painting technique using a sponge to give texture and color to the surface of a set.

STRAP HINGE—A hinge with two triangular blades by which it is fastened.

STRIKE—The term for removing scenery, props, and lights from the stage at the end of an act or of a performance.

STRIP LIGHTS—A number of lights placed together to illuminate a specific stage area, such as a doorway.

SWITCHBOARD—The panel which contains controls for all the stage lighting.

TEASERS—A special cloth border upstage of the first border lights. Used with tormentors to form an inner-picture frame, usually very ornate.

TECHNICAL DIRECTOR—The person responsible for creating a stage setting from a scenic design and for controlling the set's manipulation onstage during a performance. This person may or may not be the set designer.

THICKNESS—The pieces placed around doors, windows, and openings to give the effect of solidity.

THYROTRON—An electronic tube dimmer; a nonmechanical device for controlling intensity of light.

TIE LINES—Lines attached to the tops of drops by which the drops are attached to battens.

TIGHT-PIN BACKFLAP HINGE—A backflap hinge from which the pin holding the two halves of the hinge together cannot be removed.

TOGGLE RAIL—The center rail of a flat.

TORMENTORS—Two pieces of framed scenery hinged together, placed left and right of the stage just back of the proscenium opening. Used with a teaser to form an inner-picture frame, usually highly ornate.

TRACK—The slide or device on which a traveller curtain operates.

TRAVELLER—A stage curtain which opens from the middle to the sides of the stage. *Also* the track in which the curtain operates.

TRAVELLER BALLS OR BLOCKS—The balls or blocks in a traveller track from which the curtain is suspended.

TRIANGLE—*See* Corners or Triangles.

TRIM—The term for adjusting any hanging scenery.

TRIPS—The lines that support the arms of a cyclorama.

TUBE DIMMER—*See* Thyrotron.

VELOUR—A heavy, napped cotton material used for making cycloramas.

VIGNETTE—*See* Cut-down Set.

WAGON—A low platform on casters; used for moving scenery.

WEBBING—A heavy reinforcing tape used at the top of cloth scenery hung from battens.

WIDE-ANGLE LENS—A lens that gives a large spot of light in a short distance.

WINGS—Two pieces of scenery hinged together to stand at an angle; used in pairs left and right stage. *Also* the area outside the acting area on both sides of the stage.

WORKING CURTAIN—*See* Act Curtain.

AUTHOR'S NOTE—Stagecraft requires the use of a great variety of highly specialized items. Electrical equipment, painting supplies, stage hardware, to name but a few, are often not readily available locally. They must be ordered from companies that specialize in the sale of this material. To list even a few of these vendors would be very difficult, but there is a publication which supplies this information: *Simon's Directory of Theatrical Materials, Services and Information*, published by Package Publicity Service, 1564 Broadway, New York, N.Y. 10036. It is probably the only book of its kind.

INDEX

Act curtain. *See* Working curtain
Alternating current, 95
Amperage: definition of, 96–97; as consideration in cable size, 97; and cable capacity formula, 97
Apron: definition of, 3
Arches: pattern for, 49; construction of, 50; proportional enlargement of, 50–51; third dimension for, 51–52; clothing of, 52
Asbestos. *See* Fire curtain
Astragal, 73
Autotransformer dimmer, 103

Backdrop: definition of, 30; construction of, 33; cyc used as, 37; enlargement of sketch for, 91; lighting of, 109
Backflap hinge: on flats, 21; with stage jack, 24; with parallels, 66
Balcony spots, 111
Banister, 62. *See also* Stairs
Barn door, 107
Batten: with a set of lines, 5; for scenery, 5–6; for cycloramas, 34–35; with Dutchman, 85
Bell box, 80
Bench: construction of, 75
Birdseye lamps: kinds of, 115; uses of, 115
Bleeding colors, 83
Book ceiling, 59
Books: construction of, 75–76
Border lights: location of, 26, 105, 110; use of, in general lighting, 99; with specific lighting, 100; directional control of, 104, 105; as source of colored light, 109
Bowline knot, 20
Box set: definition of, 31; use of borders with, 31; vignette as variation of, 37–38
Brace cleat, 47
Bunch light, 105
Butt hinge, 71

Cable and wire: sizes of, 97; types of, 97–98; care of, 98

Carbon arc lights, 107
Carpentry department: responsibilities of, 28; composition of, 28
Casein paint: uses of, 75, 85; characteristics of, 83
Ceiling: definition of, 31; color of, 31; construction of, 57–58; types of, 58–59
Ceiling iron, 58
Chair: construction of, 75
Chandeliers: responsibility for, 76–77; construction of, for period plays, 77
Changing scenery. *See* Scene changing
Chicken wire. *See* Poultry netting
Clinching iron: description of, 40; use of, 44
Clothing flats: materials for, 42, 47; procedure in 47–48; gluing of edges in, 48–49
Clout nails: use of, in applying keystones and corners, 43, 44; clinching of, 44
Clovehitch, 6
Color: use of, in set decoration, 87; in panelled walls, 89; in simple interiors, 90–91; theory of, 92; effect of light on, 92–93, 113–14
Color of light: control of, 101; materials for, 108–9; uses of, 111; effect of, on colored surfaces, 113–14; on make-up and costume, 114
Company box, 96
Condenser. *See* Lens
Connectors: types of, 98
Corner or triangle: specifications for, 41–42; use of, on flats, 43–44; on parallels, 65
Corrugated cardboard: use of, in building profile scenery, 53
Costumes: responsibility for, 27; effect of colored light on, 114
Cotton line or cord: for guillotine curtain, 10; for traveller pull-off rigging, 13; for lashlines, 42
Counterweight system: operation of, 6–7; disadvantages of, 7; for fire curtain, 8–9
Cycloramas: bracing the stage door in, 24; definition of, 30; materials for, 30, 33; use of borders with, 31; types of, 32; battens for, 34–35;

128